Noah ~~~~~~~~~~~~~~~~~~~ e
from Granny

WHAT A PIECE OF WORK

WHAT A PIECE OF WORK

On Being Human

Helen Oppenheimer

imprint academic.com

Published in the UK by
Imprint Academic, PO Box 200, Exeter EX5 5YX, UK

Published in the USA by
Imprint Academic, Philosophy Documentation Center
PO Box 7147, Charlottesville, VA 22906-7147, USA

ISBN 184540 0631
ISBN-13 9781845400637
A CIP catalogue record for this book is available from the
British Library and US Library of Congress

To my niece

PATRICIA BRIMS

Contents

What a piece of work is a man! How noble in reason! How infinite in faculty! In form, in motion, how express and admirable! In action how like an angel! In apprehension how like a god! The beauty of the world! The paragon of animals! And yet, to me, what is this quintessence of dust?

Hamlet, II. ii. 309

Preface

This book is a small discussion of an enormous subject, 'What is special about human beings?' Once it might have been simply called, 'What is man?' but nowadays that would be thoughtless and indeed insensitive. What I hope to do is pursue the theme of *creation* which I took up in an earlier book called *Making Good*. I had in mind there the whole natural world, in the light of the problem of evil. Now I should like to consider more particularly living creatures, especially the creatures we ourselves are. My recurring theme is: prefer 'both/and' to 'either/or'. 'People are miserable sinners—*and* magnificent.' 'We really are animals—*and* one of these animals was Shakespeare.'

I am writing as a somewhat orthodox Christian theologian whose subject is ethics, in the hope that my point of view may be intelligible and even congenial to fellow-Christiana and some non-Christians. It would be useless to argue from authority. I believe that human beings, like all animals, are part of a created universe, but I have tried not to let my argument depend on assumptions which could not be entertained by agnostics. Rather than saying to the reader, 'This is what the Bible, or the church, teaches', I would rather offer an exploration of what Christians can believe, in the hope that it may be found persuasive. It should be constructive, not faithless, to treat the beliefs of the Bible and the church as responsible hypotheses, which could be strengthened or weakened by evidence. The shape of responsible apologetic is: 'Suppose this, then what follows? Will it hold up?'

The rather large number of references and quotations is an attempt to show gratitude to many people from whom I have learnt. Some of the people to whom I owe most are no longer there to be thanked. I must mention particularly G.R. Dunstan to whose wisdom and encouragement I owed much over the years. The Bibliography is supposed to include all the works which have even a small place in my argument, whether favourable or unfavourable, and a few more which I have found useful. I have not put in books of

the Bible; nor Collected Works of standard poets; nor isolated quotations or references for which anything more than a footnote would
be name-dropping.

I am much indebted to my son-in-law, Ivo Mosley, for constructive advice at several stages; to Michael Screech, then acting chaplain
of All Souls College, Oxford, for inviting me in June 2002 to preach
the sermon from which this book took its rise; and once again to my
husband for multifarious help.

Chapter 1

Only Human

What is man that thou art mindful of him:
  and the son of man, that thou visitest him?
Thou madest him lower than the angels:
  to crown him with glory and worship.

Psalm 8.4–5

People who complain of being misunderstood widen the gap between themselves and everybody else. If they argue, they are argumentative. If they fall silent, they are spineless. The Christian church is in this predicament, in our time and probably in most times. Christians find their good intentions ignored and their sins and follies relished. The grace they need is a combination of charity and clarity, a good deal more difficult than defensiveness.

Christians today have to face not only the ordinary accusation that their beliefs are false and misleading, but also more wounding charges of ethical insensitivity. This assault has the demoralizing effect of feeding the defeatism which says, 'It's no good: you are going to be wrong anyway.'

The attack comes from two contrary directions at once. On the one hand, Christians are assumed to be gloomily anti-humanist, so busy repenting of their sins that they cannot value human vitality, so beset by their faultiness that they cannot appreciate human achievements. On the other hand Christians are accused of taking too smugly confident a view of human worth, belittling the wonder of other creatures and assuming that only human beings matter. The 'dominion' given to Adam in the book of Genesis 'over every living thing' has seemed to license his offspring to crash around the universe in overweening arrogance, maltreating our fellow-creatures and damaging the delicate balance of nature on which, as we ought to know by now, we all depend.

Both these accusations have plausibility, even both at once. The more fashionable of the two complaints is the arrogance of human beings, a distinctive arrogance apparently sustained by religious faith. Christians can appear conceited and even heartless, because their tradition encourages them to rate human beings more highly than the other animals with whom they share the planet. Is it presumptuous to claim to be the creatures who are made 'in the image of God'? 'Anthropocentric', human-centred, invites an accusation of *self*-centredness. The ugly late-twentieth-century word 'speciesist', on the analogy of 'racist' and 'sexist', means somebody who is élitist (another unpleasing word), not about social status but about human status. This attack is too serious to be shrugged off by linguistic wriggling.

Sometimes it is asserted that the God Christians worship is irrevocably 'speciesist'. The message is coming through that it is time to grow out of our pious conviction that we were specially created at the top of a hierarchy, 'of more value than many sparrows'. Must we take our place instead as merely one kind of beast in a more democratic universe? There was a zoo which put up a notice 'The most dangerous animal' beside a doorway which led to a mirror. It would seem to be at least a half-truth that our own species is especially destructive and predatory.

This charge was deployed with particular effectiveness by Peter Singer in his classic manifesto, *Animal Liberation*. The harms human beings inflict upon animals, especially animals bred in factory farms, are relentlessly described and the practical conclusions hammered home. It must be said at once that no theologian today trying to address the ancient question 'What is man?' should dare to write in exactly the same way as if that book had never been written. It is not good enough now to presume upon our superiority.

When we rightly repudiate the notion that we are only naked apes, it is the dismissive 'only' that must be queried. We may affirm that human creatures are 'made in God's image'; but to understand what that means needs a more generous effort to relate them to the whole creation to which they belong, not one-sidedly to their Maker. The question of the moral standing of animals and the belief that animals, like people, can have interests, and maybe even rights, can no longer be ignored.

For Peter Singer, *equal* consideration for the interests of all sentient creatures is evidently non-negotiable; but his vegetarianism is not fanatical. He takes into account which creatures really are sentient.[1] He recommends realism about how far all-or-nothing recommenda-

[1]   Singer, *Animal Liberation*, 1975, e.g. pp. 174, 177, 232–3

tions could prove effective in bettering the lot of animals. If I honour and take heed of his stance, but fail either to adopt his vegetarian conviction or to prove it wrong, my position will have to be counted as 'disagreement' and not expect to be reckoned as 'compromise', but I would hope not to stand self-condemned as hopelessly hostile.

Those of us who are still not vegetarians, but understand that animal lives make moral claims upon us and matter for their own sakes not just for ours, must ourselves be realistic and not expect to find much favour with either side. To look for some sort of middle way, taking the argument about animal rights seriously and trying to be humane, without being totally converted, is to face, with meagre defences, charges of crankiness on the one hand, and worse charges of selfish prejudice on the other hand. A short answer looks like special pleading; but a defence exhaustive enough to satisfy critics would demand such resources of time and expertise as to hijack all ethical and theological enquiry about how human beings should live their lives.

There are other moral claims than animal liberation. To leave everything else aside in order to start by justifying one's present way of life would be needlessly defensive. Human relationships, human creativity, human politics allow and may indeed require that the challenge of animal rights should be set respectfully and provisionally on one side. Because human beings are sinful and ought always to repent, it may not follow that on controversial moral issues it is invariably one's duty to adopt what looks like the safer option, and desist from treating any fellow creature in a debatable way.

If specializing is not a sin, it should be allowable to make conscientious practical decisions as well as I can; and when fuller justification is required to rely upon the authority of other people whom I trust. One can examine important questions, even matters of life and death, without oneself taking every topic back to first principles or going on arguing until everyone is convinced. Theologians are not obliged to prove the existence of God to the satisfaction of atheists before they can have anything to say about the Trinity or Christian ethics.

It is not a foregone conclusion which way the onus of proof lies about the moral status of animals. Just as Christian meat-eaters ought to take conscientious heed of their duties to other creatures, so Christian vegetarians should take realistic heed of human prehistory. At least a small protest may be registered against the

assumption that meat-eating is nothing more than gluttony.[2] It is
more closely bound up with our evolution than that. 'Man' has
always been carnivorous. Human digestions are adapted for deriv-
ing their protein from meat. Of the ape-like forerunners of humanity, the lines who remained herbivorous died out. It was the line
which took up eating meat which produced offspring who were
well-nourished enough to evolve larger brains and become our
ancestors.

   Vegetarianism is a renunciation, not only of greedy pleasures of
the table, but of significant forms of common life which have some
prima facie claim not to be swept away. The explanation of our origins
given, for instance, by Richard Leakey and Roger Lewin emphasizes
the thousands of years of the hunting and gathering way of life as
giving clues to what human nature is.[3] According to their account,
the 'basic primate social pattern' was replaced with 'a uniquely
human society based on division of labor', which 'demanded a
degree of social cooperation not displayed by any of our primate
cousins' (p. 138). There is no need to make a debating point of their
assertion that 'to be a vegetarian is to be essentially solitary' (p. 140)
to acknowledge the likelihood that 'Much of what makes us human
is in us because we developed the unique habit of collecting and
sharing plant and animal foods' (p. 149).

   Although it is honourable and may be positively healthy to
become a vegetarian today, giving up meat is not simply analogous
to giving up smoking. A nearer analogy is pacifism, to which
undoubtedly some good people are called while others remain con-
scientiously unconvinced. Many of us do not think that killing animals is a kind of murder nor that eating meat is a kind of
cannibalism. Most of us do not think that we ought to refuse to
accept medical treatment based on animal experiments. Still less do
we think it right to deny antibiotics to our children, or to disapprove
of our diabetic friends depending upon insulin.

   Those of us who allow animals to be killed on our behalf may reasonably believe that dying does not have the dread meaning for any
other creature that it has for us.[4] Human beings look 'before and
after' as other animals do not. Their manifold sensitivities are morally relevant. But arguments like these do not justify abandoning

[2]   Deane-Drummond, *The Ethics of Nature*, 2004, p. 75
[3]   Leakey and Lewin, *Origins*, 1977, ch. 7
[4]   See DeGrazia, *Taking Animals Seriously*, 1996, p. 212. He asks whether death
       may harm animals less than it harms humans, urging that 'We have work to
       do.'

any active concern for the animal creation. Killing a living creature, even without any hurt, is not trivial. Hurting a sentient creature should be a painfully hard choice. Hurting a <u>sentient</u> creature point-- *capable* lessly is a moral offence. It is not too much to ask that we should set *of* limits and encourage one another to set limits. For example, one can *feeling* take heed of how one's food has been farmed. One can support causes such as the Fund for the Replacement of Animals in Medical Experiments.[5]

People have duties to animals, often neglected; and animals suffer wrongs, often ignored. Professor G.R. Dunstan had some wise words on this subject. 'The air is thick now', he said in 1982, 'with the language of rights.'[6] He believed that the interests of animals would be more fruitfully advanced with the language of duties. 'I can assert', he went on, 'that men have duties to animals, and specify them, and give good reason for my assertion, without the premise that animals have rights.' Such a middle way deserves better than to be ignored by people who do not care about animals, or scorned by people who think poorly of human beings.

It is still a <u>tenable</u> position for a somewhat traditional Christian *- held* theologian to continue to give priority to humankind. The value of *defensible,* human beings themselves, as fallen but wonderful creatures of God, *maintaining* deserves attention for its own sake. It is even possible to assert that we can, truly, be called the crown of creation.[7] This must be affirmed carefully and humbly, mindful of the harm which human pride, cruelty and thoughtlessness can do and does. Hamlet's magnificent praise of human grandeur begins, 'What a piece of work is a man!' but has to end, 'And yet, to me, what is this quintessence of dust?'

In computer jargon, it is a promising 'default position' that human beings in spite of their wicked ways are glorious creatures and that their failings are <del>aberrations</del>. Scolding one another is counterpro- *- deviation* ductive. If I believe that nobody loves me, I am bound to become less *from* and less lovable. If I am convinced that people simply are deplor- *normal,* able, I give up trying to do better myself or to encourage other people *(a)se* to do better. Pessimism is self-fulfilling: but, more happily, so is optimism.

It is worth trying out the suggestion that when people argue about whether humanity is shameful or wonderful, both sides may be right. It is an excellent rule of thumb to make a habit of saying

---

[5]   FRAME: Eastgate House, 34 Stoney Street, Nottingham, NG1 1NB
[6]   Dunstan 'Science and sensibility', 1982, pp. 11, 12 and *passim*
[7]   Oppenheimer, *Finding & Following*, 1994, p. 43

both/and rather than either/or. When it looks horribly convincing
that human beings are the worst kind of animal, it is time to remember the dictum that the worst is the *corruption* of the best, the best
gone bad. It is the very excellence of humanity which has the capacity to go dramatically wrong. Judging people's value is not a plain
matter of alternatives, like deciding whether somebody is dishonest
or honest. It is a gloomy over-simplification to write off human
beings as vile, in clear contrast to other creatures who are innocent.
'Lilies that fester smell far worse than weeds.'[8]

Human self-esteem goes bad like the self-esteem of the Pharisee in
the parable: 'Lord I thank thee that I am *not as other men* ...' . By ordinary standards he is indeed a *good* man: his merits are real and his
gratitude is real. He spoils it, not by wrongdoing, but by being negative about everybody else. Instead of generously looking out for
goodness everywhere, he sets other people's faults in contrast with
his own obedience. Likewise people who are thankful for the
wonder of humanity may, but need not, fall into dismissing other
creatures as brutes.

It is a standing temptation to make goodness competitive, not
understanding that values are variegated.[9] Good things do not
belong on a scale from better to worse. If something is to be called
excellent, this is not for winning a beauty contest between rival candidates. If the universe really is glorious, it is an abundant show of
wonders where one glory enhances another.

The way a believer will express this is, 'And God saw everything
that he had made, and, behold, it was very good.' There is no need
for a competition; or is there? The story in *Genesis* of how 'In the
beginning God created the heaven and the earth' does suggest a progression from good to best. The narrative arrives at a summit, the
creation of humankind, male and female. Human beings come at the
place of honour at the end: at which point they are expressly given
'dominion' over all the other creatures. Much animal suffering has
come from the abuse of this privilege.

Christians who have become aware that 'man's dominion' poses
an ethical question try to explain it or to explain it away. One way
they ought not to deal with the problem is to discount the authority
of their scriptures. That would be to cut off the branch they are sitting
on. By all means let historians call the story that God created mankind from the dust of the earth, on the sixth day, a *myth*. The story is

[8]   Shakespeare, Sonnet 94
[9]   Oppenheimer, *Making Good,* 2001, ch. 5

told in picture language; but the question is whether the message it conveys is true. The gist of the story seems to be this: that the universe derives its being from God and that the existence and character of human beings derive from God's purposes. But if 'mythical' has to mean 'fictitious' and the arrival of humankind is not to be affirmed as the climax of the process of creation, then the redemption of humankind, Part II of the story, loses credibility likewise. The New Testament has its roots so deeply entwined with the Hebrew scriptures that the Gospel could hardly survive being simply uprooted. Some kind of primacy for human beings seems to be an integral part of the biblical statement.

The culmination of the narrative in *Genesis* 1 is the creation of human beings: 'So God created humankind in his own image.'[10] The more ancient account in the next chapter tells, more specifically and one can say more naively, that God shaped a man out of clay and then brought him to life with his breath.[11] That is indeed picture language. Even if believers used to be convinced that in historical fact the first man was moulded in the shape of a God with head and hands and feet, most of them have long since moved on to greater sophistication.

The doctrine that people are created to be like God has been refined, not abandoned. For Christians, the likeness is rooted in God's love, from which human love derives. They can base their understanding of the image of God upon the doctrine of the Trinity.[12] If God is not a solitary Power but three Persons who are One, then love is built into God's very nature. To believe that human beings are like their Maker is to believe that love is built into human nature.

The old stories presuppose that the universe was created according to God's good purpose. They appears to presuppose just as fundamentally that humanity is the goal of the entire process. Of all the living creatures which God has called into being, it is only humankind which is said to be made in God's own image. Before questions about animal rights came into focus, Christian enquiry about how to specify the meaning of the 'image of God' concentrated unselfcons-

---

[10] *Genesis* 1.27 (ascribed to the Priestly writer who collected and arranged the traditions after the Exile).

[11] *Genesis* 2.7 (ascribed to the much earlier Yahwist writer, so called from the use of 'Yahweh' as God's Name.) See Oppenheimer, 2001, p. 53.

[12] The way the idea of the image of God is 'amplified' by the doctrine of the Trinity is brought out clearly in Dunstan's Malcolm Millar Lecture, 1981, 'Therapy and care', pp. 6–7.

ciously upon this biblical contrast between human beings and animals.

Belief in human superiority is strongly entrenched. For Christians, the presuppositions both of scripture and of scientific understanding seem to coincide to maintain it. The Bible promises mankind dominion over the rest of creation. There is no surprise here, because people can see for themselves that human beings are cleverer than animals. They readily claim the right to rule over the animals and make them serve human purposes.

The assumption of supremacy seemed straightforward when animals were brutes and man was master. But now, in reaction against ancient oppressions, it is questionable whether any creature may be put above any other. Women, different races, primitive societies, people with disabilities, and now animals are to come into their own. The tradition of drawing a sharp line between man and beast has been dented. Biblical scholars who look carefully find that the Biblical evidence about 'man's dominion' is more complicated. Meanwhile the study of animal life suggests that these other creatures have a greater moral status than human beings have liked to suppose.

So far, so good: but the more the intrinsic value of animals is recognized, the more the discussion about animal rights polarizes and turns into a debate. People who have been half convinced begin to say, 'Oh but surely …'. They may have no worked-out case against animal rights, but they instinctively feel that all this is going too far. If the Lord ate the Passover lamb without demur, who are we to improve upon his example? Egalitarianism may be all very well, but surely it stops with humanity?

People who remain unconverted to treating animals simply as equals are not thereby shown up as cruel, selfish or even lazy. Deeply ingrained in our ordinary ways of thinking is the certainty that human beings simply are more *important* than animals. Of course animals matter morally. People should be concerned about animals, even greatly concerned; but this can still be seen as an obligation to be kind rather than an obligation to recognise animal rights. In olden days people might get out of their carriage and walk up a steep slope to spare the horses. That is very different from letting the horses choose whether to take the job of pulling the carriage or not.

When ancient confidence in human dominion is questioned, discussion becomes argument and argument separates like curdled

mayonnaise. Declarations of animal rights meet reaffirmations of
human superiority. John W. Funder, a medical research worker
doing tough surgical experiments on animals, briskly defended
human prerogatives 'because *Animal Liberation* was written by Peter
Singer, and not by a chimpanzee; because the RSPCA is staffed by
people, not dolphins'.[13]

Answers cannot be found if the discussion remains so polarized.
Traditionalists take their stand on commonsense, but find their
assumptions swept aside as insensitive. Advocates of animal rights
assume that the high moral ground is theirs and alienate the people
they want to convince, who begin to feel as if they were being put in
the wrong by definition. Still more when animal liberation takes
the counter-productive form of violent attacks on human beings,
traditionalists feel thoroughly justified in carrying on as they
always have.

Can we do better than bandying debating points on one side or the
other which defeat without convincing? The disagreement is recalcitrant, because it is a matter of contrary intuitions. Is it obvious, or a
deep-rooted prejudice, that people matter more than beasts? Is it
ethical, or merely quarrelsome, to demand a fundamental reap-
praisal of human attitudes to non-human animals? Partisanship one
way or the other looks easier than realizing the strength of the contrary case; but since I find myself on both sides at once I must not
enlist on one side or the other. To persist in saying 'both/and', own-
ing two points of view simultaneously, requires a considerable but
worthwhile effort.

Once upon a time moralists would recommend that people who
want to know what their duties really are should turn to *casuistry*.
Casuistry properly means 'The art or science of bringing general
principles to bear upon particular cases.'[14] When small weights are
added carefully to one side or the other, presently the scales will tip.
Granted certain undisputed duties such as justice and kindness,
how do these apply or not apply to the ways people ought to treat
other creatures?

The right use of casuistry should require a conscientious effort to
follow the argument wherever it goes. In practice, casuistry is easily
misused by people who want to steer the argument one way rather
than another. Carefully to set out possible considerations is a favour-

[13] Funder, 'Experiments on animals in medical research', 1989, p. 14
[14] *The Oxford Dictionary of the Christian Church*, 1997, p. 297. See also Preston,
      'Christian ethics', 1991, p. 94

ite strategy. To justify themselves for going on doing what they have happily been allowed to do so far, they fasten on debating points to uphold their preconceptions. So casuistry has acquired a not wholly undeserved bad name for encouraging legalism, or special pleading, or both. It is fair to say that in addressing complex problems, legalism may have its uses; but special pleading is just what authentic casuistry seeks to avoid. People who have become aware of moral questions ought not to short-circuit them by taking sides first and then looking for arguments in self-justification.

When I am defensively anxious about the way human beings treat animals, I may triumphantly notice free-range hens huddling together in the muddy corner of a field, not ranging freely. The cruelty of batteries is not thereby refuted. Likewise an individual slave owner on the defensive might sincerely have said, 'I look after my slaves well'; but the institution of slavery was not vindicated. This is where the argument ought to start, not stop.

There is evidently some analogy between factory farming and slavery. What ought to be done about it? This means, not 'How can I justify myself?' but 'What ought I to do or stop doing?' For some people all-or-nothing stands are attractive. They ought to bear in mind the practical word 'counterproductive'. The more they argue about rights and wrongs, the more they risk inducing a kind of 'blame fatigue'.

When people lose patience with being constantly put in the wrong, it is simple but superficial to defend ingrained human prejudice by making debating points to mock the unwelcome notion of people owing duties to animals. If more creatures than 'man' matter morally, where do we draw the line? Is it murder or self-defence to kill a wasp? Since the smallpox virus is a creature of God, why should it not be protected, like the pink pigeon, from following the dodo into extinction? Is it mammals who count? That is where Peter Singer sets the boundary: so are we to think of insects, reptiles and plants as without moral status, though we may find them beautiful or useful? Of course these awkward questions are self-interested, but they are not silly. To brush them aside is superficial too. It still may be asked, and needs to be asked, how fundamental are the differences between human beings and other animals. Are we really special and if we are, what makes us so?

To ask that question is itself characteristically human. Among our particular characteristics, indeed responsibilities, is drawing lines and making distinctions. We must analyse and clarify. At the same time we must hold on firmly to the connection between 'human' and 'humane'. We are required to put our hearts as well as our minds into finding out what to think about ourselves and other creatures. Such moral concern is not childish nor eccentric. Sympathy need not slip into sentimentality, any more than analysis need slip into callousness.

Whatever judgements we proceed to make, it must be a relevant fact that we share 98% of our DNA with chimpanzees.[15] What the crucial 2% has done for us can be better appreciated when we are willing to marvel at how small it is. People's understanding of creation's glory is enriched when they learn to take into account other kinds of creatures than human beings. It should be a liberating not a threatening belief that animals too have value in their own right and not only because they are useful or pleasing to us.

---

[15] See e.g. Diamond, *The Rise and Fall of the Third Chimpanzee*, 1991, pp. 46–7

Chapter 2

Appreciation

The question is not, Can they reason? nor Can they talk? but
Can they suffer?

Jeremy Bentham
Introduction to the Principles of Morals and Legislation,1789, ch. 17

It is natural for human beings to assume that evolution has a direction, leading upwards to *homo sapiens* as the most remarkable of all
the animals. We should be critical, but not dismissive, of this conviction. It has come to sound shocking, because human beings have
presumed upon it. 'These people are like animals' is used as a simple
insult. The characteristics some people perceive in animals are
aggression and violence; instinctive behaviour guided by no forethought; and, perhaps especially, filth and squalor. It has been
customary to despise the 'brute beasts that have no understanding'.[1]

'Beast' does not have to be a term of abuse, but people are more
prone to call one another 'beastly' than to affirm with the Psalmist,
'Thou, Lord, shalt save both man and beast'. The more politically
correct translation, 'You save humans and animals alike, O Lord' ,
has not given rise to much reflection upon what kind of salvation
might apply to animals. The argument about humanity and the
other creatures has been allowed to become and remain polarized.

People who would rather take a middle way, who are convinced
that other concerns matter as well as animal rights, are not excused,
nor are they disqualified, from taking animal wrongs to heart.
Human beings ought to consider with an open mind what their
duties to the rest of creation may be. They should be ready to take
heed and to take trouble: to be, for instance, more humane consumers. They are not hypocritical if they still believe that the challenge of
'animal liberation' can be pressed too far.

The weighty proponents of animal rights may be challenged in
their turn. If they are overstating their case, they must be criticized in

one who argues in favor of something

[1] The Solemnisation of Matrimony in the *Book of Common Prayer*

detail; but first there is a more general criticism to make, that they are putting their case in a misleading way. There is plenty of sincere moral fervour about animal suffering, much of it well founded; but the form it takes may be unconstructive. This dissatisfaction with the 'animal rights' case is hard to explain fairly, because it has to be an argument from silence, from what is not being said. It is difficult to prove anything from negative data.

What often fails to come into full view is the positive perception about animals that they matter for their own sake as our fellow creatures.[2] The reformers tend to concentrate, understandably enough, on what is deplorably wrong. Sometimes they are even at pains to deny that they are 'animal lovers', for fear that their - austerely moral point of view will be identified with sentimentality. They do not say much to invite distinct appreciation of these other living beings whose cause they have taken up. It is no wonder that traditionalists set up a resistance to all the moralizing. They are being driven on to the defensive, not led into an understanding of what they are missing. So the argument remains polarized and the particular excellences of both animals and people slip quietly out of view.

It could be more telling than relentlessly pursuing the attack to stand back and marvel at creatures who, like us, are 'fearfully and wonderfully made'.[3] Then we might see and feel that their treatment matters. It would not be fair to criticize books on ethics for not being books on ethology; but consideration of what animals are really like may do more to summon up the humanity of human beings than persistent emphasis on human selfishness. Emphasis on rights, needful as it may be, can even block out lively concern for the living creatures who bear the rights. To think about real animals and attend to what the people who understand them have to say encourages appreciation.

People who are natural animal lovers find it easy to see the animals' side. They will be inclined to read the books. People who lack this spontaneous enthusiasm are resistant to argumentation, and still more resistant to preaching, about their neglected duties. Nagging is like jamming on the brakes on slippery ground. The advice for people who want to travel safely is paradoxical: to steer into the skid. Alice in Looking-glass Land found that the most direct way towards the garden of live flowers always led her back to the house, and what she had to do was set off in what looked like the wrong direction.

---

[2]   See Sharpe, *Creatures Like Us?*, 2005
[3]   *Psalm* 139.13

A path which explores the excellence of *humanity* might appear to be most evidently heading in the wrong direction. Perhaps this route might work as well as it did for Alice. Instead of trying to be fair to animals by concentrating on human sinfulness, what about starting paradoxically in the opposite direction, by celebrating human beings themselves? Willingness to consider what human glory could be might make one not less but more capable of valuing creatures of all kinds.

The pendulum has swung and the roundabouts have turned, and human beings are discouraged now from thinking of themselves as the crown of creation. It is a shame if we have therefore come to feel no kind of grateful wonder at the way our own capacities have developed. There comes a time for taking notice of distinctively human achievement. Just as parents rightly marvel at the attainment of their toddler who is learning to talk, so it is right for developed *homo sapiens* to marvel at the achievements of our early ancestors, at the excellence of palaeolithic cave paintings and the elegance of Solutrian flint hand axes.

There must have been two-legged hominids who first wondered about their place in the universe, even though they were not called Adam and Eve. Somebody must have first recognized, long before Kant, 'the starry heavens above and the moral law within'.[4] This wonder itself was marvellous.

It cannot be emphasized too strongly that appreciation is positive and does not depend upon belittling everything else. When people are moved to praise, they are not setting up a contrast with blame. To say 'What a piece of work is a man!' is no insult to the singing of skylarks, the proverbially long memories of elephants, the engineering work of beavers, the devotion of spaniels, the industry of ants, the gracefulness of antelopes, or the 'fearful symmetry' of tigers.[5] Bishop Butler said, 'Everything is what it is, and not another thing'.[6] The universe has room for incommensurable blessings.

Such a comprehensive emphasis on the variegated wonder of creation is neither newfangled nor foreign to our tradition. From the morning stars singing together and the Leviathan taking his pastime, to the lilies of the field beautifully arrayed, Christians have plenty of authority for considering the natural world. A.M. Allchin commended the Eastern Christian attitude to the lives of other

[4]   Kant, *Critique of Practical Reason*, 1788
[5]   William Blake, The Tyger
[6]   Butler, *Fifteen Sermons Preached at the Rolls Chapel*, Preface

animals; and from this perspective he likewise saw 'nothing eccentric or sentimental' about the dealings of St Francis with his fellow creatures.[7] The world of nature is the context in which human excellence belongs.

Proper appreciation of people, animals, or any kind of creature needs *discrimination*, which should mean the attentive discernment of whatever is there to be found. To be *un*discriminating is to be incapable of careful discernment. Unfortunately 'discrimination' has almost lost its affirmative meaning by taking on an official antagonistic use. It has come to mean something like 'putting down'. People discriminate *against* other people, contrasting rather than comparing. They lose touch with both/and. They set about selecting successful candidates by eliminating the inadequate candidates who fail the test, rather than by approving the good ones. Then it becomes apparent, not only to the rejected candidates, that some tests are arbitrary and the discriminations they make are unfair. Unhappily but inexorably the good meaning of 'discrimination' is tarnished. It ceases to be a kind of wise judgment, and becomes an objectionable, nowadays even illegal, way of making false judgments. Discrimination is diagnosed as a moral offence, snobbery at best, heartless selfishness at worst. Equality, for good and ill, is recognized as a more promising 'default position' than glory for some.

It is coming to be understood that we are not to discriminate against people for being male or female, dark-skinned or fair, highly or humbly born, rich or poor, clever or stupid. These are not relevant to people's moral standing. What then about being *homo sapiens* or a gorilla? Is it unfair discrimination against animals, or proper discernment, to emphasize the differences between people and other living creatures as differences of kind, not just differences of degree? The question cannot be postponed for long, whether human beings really have unique moral status, and if so, by what right? We are happy to affirm that each person is sacred; but then what should we add, by comparison or contrast, about the sacredness of animals?

Traditionally there has been a plain answer, that the sacredness of persons is to be confidently identified with the sacredness of their immortal *souls*. Christians have assumed that what is special about human beings is something—some thing—that we have and 'the beasts that perish' do not. Christian faith has been sure that because

[7]   Allchin, 'The theology of nature in the eastern fathers and among Anglican theologians', 1975, p. 147. See Linzey and Cohn-Sherbok, *After Noah: Animals and the Liberation of Theology*, 1997.

human creatures have souls they alone can indeed survive the death of their bodies.

In trying to explain their heavenly hopes, Christians have too hastily combined belief in God, belief in life after death and belief in the philosophical notion of the immortality of the soul as if they all stood or fell together. Of these, only belief in God has always been part of the tradition of God's people. The ancient Israelites generally aspired to live on by having many descendants. Later on, to assert individual existence beyond death was to side with the Pharisees, against the Sadducees who denied an afterlife. The distinctively firm Christian belief in heaven was founded on the resurrection of Christ. Succeeding generations of believers came to ask, when they reasoned about their faith, how it could be make sense to say that people can live when their earthly bodies die. The Greek idea of immortal souls offered a promising answer. Christians have not always realised that to allow the immortality of the soul to take over from the resurrection of the body means stepping out of the ancient Hebrew tradition that what God created was whole persons.

The enquiry about the value and sacredness of humanity has often taken the form, '*Do* human beings have souls?' This is or should be a question of fact. It needs to be distinguished from the question of value, which asks what matters about humanity, whether and how humankind is wonderful. If the sacredness of human creatures is taken to be entirely summed up by their being the only ones with souls, enquiry about the value and sacredness of the rest of God's creation may go by default.

Much of the vocabulary used in this discussion is potentially ambiguous. If human or animal life is sacred, it might follow, sternly, that it is never to be destroyed, or more vaguely that it is never to be treated casually. Sacredness, moral status, importance, mattering all need to be applied watchfully if they are not to slip into saying what is not meant.

All these words are used to *commend*. They express some sort of approval, but they do not have to assert simply, 'This is on a higher moral footing'. Suppose we want to affirm that people but not butterflies have *ethical status*, we are not therefore praising the people and censuring the butterflies. We are judging, rightly or wrongly, that insects should be classified with plants or machines, not with saints and sinners.

When people say that trees are *important*, they are not making a moral judgement that it is cruel to hurt them. They are none the less

making value judgements: that trees are beautiful and life-enhancing;
or, more threateningly, that rain forests are vital to the well-being of
the planet. These are aesthetic or economic affirmations: though
undoubtedly moral consequences will follow from them.

Even when the words we use for commending have direct and
unambiguous moral significance, they may still suggest misleading
implications. To assert that something *matters* makes a positive
moral point. It must be emphasized and reiterated that other things
are not to be therefore disparaged as not mattering. We know that
human pain is important. We should not need to mark it up by
marking animal pain down. Commending has no need to be set in
relief by blaming.

Taking animal suffering into serious account means being recep-
tive to the commonsense belief that animals really do have the feelings they seem to have. They are not merely a backdrop to human
life. Their pain does matter in its own right. What determines how
much it matters is not what human beings feel about it, but whether
and how seriously the animals themselves are capable of *minding*.
Bentham's challenge (on page 14 above) ought to be the model:
'Can they suffer?' It is both natural and just to make use of the same
criterion both for human and for animal pain: how much does this
creature mind?

Another classic book, Tom Regan's *The Case for Animal Rights* , has
gone further than this and argued in great detail, not only that
animals have moral status, but that they should be counted equally
with human beings. The criterion is whether this creature is the
subject of a life. One might say, has it a biography? Is it aware of
different experiences happening one after another, some welcome
and others unwelcome? An amoeba is alive but has no spark of 'me'
about it, whereas one can wonder quite sensibly whether chimpanzees or dogs might be even be thought of as persons. Somewhere in
between amoebae and people come chickens and rabbits, and
maybe human infants. The line Regan draws, without explaining
exactly why, is that anyway any mammal of more than a year old is a
'subject of a life'. He believes that the interests of such an animal,
whatever these turn out to be, ought to be given the same respect as
the interests of a human being, a respect which amounts to full
ethical status. He insists that this kind of inherent value is not a
matter of more or less. 'It does not come in degrees.'[8]

_____

[8]   Regan, *The Case for Animal Rights*, 2004, pp. 240–1 and e.g. pp. 236, 247

At least the conclusion should be fully accepted, that animals are more important for their own sakes than people have liked to imagine, and that their pain, discomfort and fear matter morally. It is still fair to take into account, on the other hand, that most animals do not 'look before and after' enough to suffer in some of the ways human beings do. They cannot experience death as 'the last enemy'.[9] Though they mind their dying, they do not mind their mortality. To say that a slaughtered ox, over and above whatever it has suffered in the abattoir, has had all its preferences frustrated and has been deprived of its whole future is true, but does not quite establish that each ox is an irreplaceable individual who has the right to go on living. The relevance of these considerations for farmers and the consumers of their products, and for laboratory scientists, is evident though not necessarily straightforward.

There are many reasons, good and bad, for harming other living creatures. Some people renounce all such persuasions and become vegetarians or pacifists, or oppose abortion or capital punishment. Others believe, variously, that there may be humane farming, a just war, a lawful release from an intolerable predicament or a needful deterrent. These convictions overlap though they do not always combine. They are more weighty when they recognize the strength of both sides of the arguments.

It is no wonder that people come to different conclusions. It is hard to find out how much suffering we are causing, even to other human beings. Acknowledged harm is difficult to weigh against other considerations about what good will come. When we take the sacredness of any kind of life seriously, we cannot therefore expect to be provided with reliable rules of thumb to tell us what we are allowed to do. What we may hope is to enhance our perception of what we are really doing.

Another way of indicating appreciation is to single something out as 'preferable'. Like mattering, preference is a source of moral ambiguities. Things can matter, and things can be preferred, in various ways. Whether or not it is in order to prefer any kind of creature to any other may not be a plain moral question. We commend impartiality; but still it is not outrageous to have a partiality for one's own kind, to prefer human beings, in the same way as one has an allowable partiality for one's own family. Richard Hare[10] pointed out that 'we get stirred up about the goodness of men because we are men'

[handwritten margin note: being on both sides]

---

[9]   *I Corinthians* 15.26
[10]   Hare, *The Language of Morals*, 1952, p. 25

This is not because only human beings count, but because we have to start where we are and work outwards from there. 'The danger', said John Benson, 'in the attempt to eliminate partial affections is that it may remove the source of all affections.'[11]

Nor is it outrageous to have a partiality for a good specimen of its kind, to value a scholar or an athlete or a bonny child. A horse is a noble animal and a lion is the king of beasts. What is objectionable is to suppose that the good that one happens to appreciate is the only kind of good; or to suppose that creatures we have not preferred are truly inferior.

When these ambiguities have been sorted out, there is a further insidious trap to avoid. Even for the sake of honouring other people's preferences, it is perilous to go so far as kind-heartedly to call good what really is not good, not preferable at all. Some scholars are cleverer than others, but shoddy work should not be called scholarly. Not many animals can fly, but a lark which cannot fly is not 'just as good' as Shelley's skylark. The excellence of animals does not include talking; but an adult human being who cannot talk is a diminished human being.

There is a tendency among liberals today to aspire to an undiffer-entiated tolerance which is hard to criticize without falling into cal-lousness. This may take the form of insisting that because nobody is to be belittled, therefore no kind of disability ought to be lamented except for the ways we disable each other. Because 'handicap' has so often been contrasted unkindly with 'normality', the contrast itself is now suspect. To be blind has to be as acceptable as to see. Because God is no respecter of persons, it looks incorrect for the Son of God to make the lame to walk. Providing a deaf child with a cochlear implant, instead of encouraging her to sign and other people to learn her language, is supposed to be insensitive in the same way as denying Welsh people their own culture expressed in the Welsh tongue. It has been suggested[12] that to dare to prefer mentally 'normal' people to people with mental disabilities is simply a disqualification to any claim to care about disabled people.

Here is a sharp example of the ambiguity of 'prefer'. It confuses what one finds congenial, what one is willing to take trouble over and what one decides is best. An expectant mother is not wrong to prefer, even greatly to prefer, that her baby will be 'normal'. If, as may happen, she comes to love her disabled child best, she does not

[11] Benson, 'Duty and the beast', 1978, p. 536
[12] Fairbairn, 'Complexity and the value of lives', 1991

have to be glad that things happened so. It should not need to be said that we should honour and celebrate with all our might the people who endure and cope with disabilities, without falling into the cruel notion that their very disabilities ought to be celebrated.

These distinctions matter for what we think as well as for how we behave. To be suspicious of people's perceptions of notable value leads into the well-meaning frame of mind for which excellence is dangerous. The keyword is 'celebrate' and what matters is to keep it positive. There need be no arrogance, still less insensitivity, about rejoicing in all manner of excellence, including the excellence of humanity. It must be possible to embark upon celebrating human beings while remaining realistic about the limitations of celebration. It would be insensitive to ignore the misfortunes of all creatures or the sinfulness of people. The hope would be that sober and grateful praise of human glory could encourage, not undermine, generous-spirited awareness of the glory, and the well-being, of other creatures.

Chapter 3
Excellence

I am a human being: I count nothing human foreign to me

Terence, *Heauton Timoroumenos*

The simplest way to dissociate oneself from ancient prejudice in our own favour is a negative way: to stop celebrating humanity. 'We human beings are just miserable sinners and the way we treat our fellow creatures is one more example.' The new orthodoxy that human beings are not special may have a Christian sound; but if it has to pull up the Christian Gospel from its Hebrew roots in God's good creation, it does not look like a proper development of the biblical tradition.

If Christian theology is an uprooted plant, it cannot be expected to produce fruit nourished by the ancestral faith of the people of God. It is fair to look at a different comparison. Plant life is not the only analogy for the growth of a tradition. Another natural way in which living things develop is by metamorphosis. Tadpoles become frogs. Christians who have adopted the Hebrew scriptures as their own have sometimes been inclined to see the newness of the Gospel as a metamorphosis of Jewish tradition, in which discontinuity may look more obvious than continuity.

The new covenant has seemed to have a different starting point from the old covenant: not creation but redemption. The Bibles of Christians start with 'Let there be light', but 'the beginning of the Gospel' is 'repent'.[1] The ancient glory of God's created work can appear to have been overwhelmed by human sinfulness. On this basis, the only human glory is trust in God's mercy. 'God saw that it was good' has given place to, 'he will save his people from their sins'. Far from standing on the foundation of creation's goodness, people are invited to a more sombre faith: not to rejoice that they are made in God's image, but to reckon themselves as repentant sinners.

---

[1] *Genesis* 1.3; *Mark* 1.1,4,15

The trouble with taking this mandatory humility as the whole story is that it shuts its eyes to real excellence, ungrateful to the Creator who endowed us with this excellence. It is as important as ever to maintain that both sides in this argument about human value are right. Both/and is still better than either/or. There is more than one valid way of looking at what human creatures are like.

On the one hand, we can start by being humble about human failings and horrified by human faults: and then still recognize and celebrate human glory. On the other hand, we can start with the affirmation that we are made in the image of God: and then still remember that our status gives us no licence for pride. We should celebrate humanity, but on condition that the break interposed by sin between our making and our saving is first fully acknowledged. The gap is wide but not unbridgeable. The new covenant encourages us to deny neither glory nor failure, but to go on asking what place there may be for human excellence in Christian ethics.

There is a lot of construction work to be done in order to hold up a positive though humble understanding of our value and the manifold ways in which human creatures may glorify God. Before human excellences can be celebrated wholeheartedly as part of the goodness of the creation, the concept of excellence itself as relevant to Christian life needs to be rehabilitated. How can we call this creature excellent without being dismissive of that one?

When excellence and equality are used as rival slogans, abandoning 'both/and', either of them can become a way of cutting some of God's creatures down to size. If excellence is given priority, the ones who are not called excellent seem to be merely inferior. But if equality is all that matters, what room is there for excellence? The deadening assumption takes hold that 'equality', means 'not standing out', as if insignificance were an important Christian value.

It is high time to take a firm grip of the idea that diversity need not imply that some must be better and others worse. Values are more valuable if they are incomparable. Honouring excellence when we find it need not mean allotting marks as if God's creatures were candidates in a competitive examination. Multiple merits need not be in opposition. Strength and gracefulness, patience and energy, intelligence and artistry, are all the more excellent for being incommensurable.

A moratorium on denigration could be a first step in making room for an effective concept of variegated worthwhileness.[2] An agreeable and not infrequent theme of the Italian Renaissance is St Francis

---

[2]   See Oppenheimer, 2001, ch. 5

and St Dominic meeting one another, not in rivalry but celebrating one another's glory, to the glory of God.[3] Unfortunately praise and blame are more often made to take turns. Valuing one creature is taken as devaluing another. If human beings are rational animals, other animals have to be irrational. But we have misunderstood the examination question we are set. It is not, 'place the following in order of merit', but 'compare and contrast'. Valuing humankind need not mean setting ourselves on a lonely pedestal. God's other diverse creatures are part of the picture.

One could at least give up saying that an unpleasing human being is 'like an animal' in a dismissive way to mean what has been meant by 'brutish'. The way some human beings behave can still be compared with some sorts of natural animal behaviour. Human faithfulness may be like the fidelity of a dog. A human artisan may be as industrious as a bee; or, conversely, as idle as a sloth. Some people are like some animals by being fierce and dangerous, or elegant and well co-ordinated, or patiently persistent, or unable to consider likely consequences, or governed by immediate impulse, or wallowing in the dirt. These comparisons with other creatures may characterize individuals quite justly, so long as they are kept specific and are never supposed to be the whole story of what either people or animals are like.

Alongside the human tendency to glorify one form of life only by belittling another, a more constructive approach has been gaining ground. Mary Midgley has pointed out vigorously that different creatures have different aims and therefore develop different capacities. For example,

> Primates do not have big cooperative enterprises, nor therefore the loyalty, fidelity, and developed skills that go with them ... But the hunting carnivores do ... And no mammal really shares the strong visual interest that is so important both to our social life and to our art, nor perhaps needs to work as hard as we do to rear our young. But birds do. This is why it is vacuous to talk of 'the difference between man and animal' without saying *which* animal.[4]

More recently, in a collection called *Animals on the Agenda*, Dorothy Yamamoto[5] has emphasized that animal lives 'may differ from ours in ways we have not yet imagined'. Therefore we can 'liberate

---

[3]   E.g. a lunette by Andrea del Sarto in the Loggia di S. Paolo in Florence.
[4]   Midgley, *Beast and Man*, 1979
[5]   Yamamoto, 'Patrolling the boundary', 1998, p. 84

them into their own, idiosyncratic ways of being' recognizing indeed that they are 'even there for their own sake'.

A possibly unfair comparison can usefully illustrate the way thinking has moved on. Only fifty years ago, C.H. Dodd, in his great book *The Fourth Gospel*, discussed what the image of God means by describing 'man' as 'something more than an offspring of the cosmos.' He explained that human beings bear God's image directly, 'not merely as the lower animals and the rest of the cosmos do, by being rationally ordered'.[6] His description of humanity as sharing in God's own mind, as even in some sense divine, can still illuminate what human beings are created to be; but today people may be distracted by the negative 'merely' for the 'lower animals'.

Other creatures ought not to be discounted as if they were inferior in God's sight. Equality prevails as the 'default position' for setting our ethical computers. It stands as a negative requirement, repudiating conceit. But the role of excellence is positive. Creatures have their own particular glories. They fulfil their capabilities by diverse excellences, which are to be looked for everywhere and celebrated in many forms.

Some of us still find ourselves possessed of a unshiftable conviction that humanity as such is of utmost importance. It is indeed: so long as we keep a firm hold of both/and. We can repudiate the arrogance which belittles other creatures without falling into gloom about the creatures we are. It would be a shame to be so afraid of 'humanism' as to ignore the wonderful excellence of human beings. If such appreciation is 'humanist', then there must be a Christian humanism. If it were contrary to Christian faith to set store by our own species, that would constitute an obstacle to Christian faith. Loyalty to humanity is one aspect of loyalty to the Christ who took human flesh, not a rebellion against him. There need be nothing particularly pagan about Terence's affirmation, '*Homo sum: humani nil a me alienum puto*', 'I am a human being: I count nothing human foreign to me'. It may be beyond us but it is not beneath us.

For some people, 'Christian humanist' is an oxymoron: a humanist is not a friend, but a foe, who puts belief in humanity in opposition to belief in God. This usage would have seemed strange to the early humanists, whose distinguishing classical learning was far from incompatible with Christian faith: but words do shift their meanings, often inconveniently. 'Humanist' in most contexts no longer means 'Greek scholar'. Stubbornly to insist on preserving a

[6]   Dodd, *The Fourth Gospel*, 1953, p. 27

once serviceable but obsolescent usage becomes misleading as well as pedantic. A more promising way forward is to find and emphasize a more central meaning of 'humanist' than either a classical scholar or a sceptic. To be a humanist, whether believing or unbelieving, is to value and appreciate human beings as wonderful: a Christian humanist will say, as wonderful creatures.

To propose such a benign significance for 'humanism' is the beginning of another argument, still not a conclusion. 'Christian humanism' is a live option, which need not be ruled out by definition: but will it do? Can loyal Christians wholeheartedly celebrate human glory? It is not obvious how a humanistic ethic of gratitude for the excellences of human beings can fit into the teaching of Christ. For Christians 'excellence' is dangerous. Rather, they recognize as a basic principle that human achievements are under judgment and that it is the smallest and weakest, who make no claims, who are to inherit the kingdom. If that sounds like the survival of the *un*fittest, then so much the worse for secular notions of what is 'fit'.

Christian humanists can cheerfully agree, indeed they should emphasize, that human value is not free-standing. It is not in their own right that human beings are excellent. Appreciative humanism does not imply self-assured individualism. Human virtues, kindness, wisdom, courage, or self-restraint, are *both* truly excellent *and* entirely dependent upon the grace of God. So far, so good.

A more difficult challenge to a humanist Christian faith is the plausibly humble conviction that human worth, however substantial it seems to us, is simply too small to have any value in the sight of the Creator. To be confident that the glory of human achievement matters looks like *vain*glory. How much wiser to follow the well-trodden path, which pursues unquestioning faith and treats scholarly intellect and inspired imagination as distractions. So must we suppose that the construction of logical arguments is presumptuous, and the fashioning of works of art even idolatrous? Scientists and painters who are Christians may search their scriptures in vain for any decisive validation of their vocations. The beauty of God's creation is frequently celebrated in the Bible, but the glories of human intellect and human artistry seem no more than ancillary at best. Must saints outgrow these enthusiasms as children outgrow their teddy bears?

Christian as this deprecation may sound, honest artists and scholars simply know that their callings are real and are not imaginary, infantile nor self-indulgent, still less sinful. They are certain that their tasks are objectively laid upon them. Their creative integrity is compulsory, not compulsive. To disown this would be something like the sin against the Holy Ghost. The pleasure and inspiration human beings find in one another's creativity and discernment is likewise not an indulgence and may be a heavenly gift.

Let it be said that the historical picture of what Christian believe is not so entirely negative. Faith and human endeavour are not always at odds. The impious scientist is a misleading stereotype. At many times the church has encouraged the visual arts with no nagging feelings of guilt. To glorify God in words is a prized gift even among puritans. The Bible itself is full of poetry. Karl Barth, renowned as he was for repudiating humanism, was far from deaf to the glory of Mozart's music. Christians may be encouraged to respond to such positive indications that human intelligence and human creativity can be aspects of the image of God.

Chapter 4

Fellow Creatures

For all the beasts of the forest are mine:
and so are the cattle upon a thousand hills.

Psalm 50.10

Suppose we are minded to celebrate humanity: what may we cele-brate? The question has been taken to mean, how are human beings superior to all these others who also are described as 'very good'? The traditional answer is that what sets us apart from the beasts is *reason*. So man, the rational animal, has appeared as the crowning glory of creation. Here has been identified our likeness to our Maker and therefore our claim to be the top creature. Indeed, our immortal soul, something which no animal has been allowed to have, has been confidently located here.

To identify reason as one particular excellence of human beings does not bring the enquiry to an end. The declaration that 'man is the rational animal' is not the whole story of people's value in the eyes of their Maker, nor the only story about the meaning of 'God saw that it was good'. Some would say that that 'Man the thinker' is a story which has been unfortunately over-valued. Instead of making rea-son pre-eminent, or even celebrating reason alongside many kinds of value, many people would rather cut rationality down to size. Reason is not allowed to be glorified, any more than Power, or Nobil-ity, or Wealth, or Beauty.

Among many kinds of snobbery, intellectual snobbery is picked out as a bad example. To praise brainpower is 'discrimination' in the current bad sense.[1] To say, 'He is an intellectual' suggests that he is both arrogant and out of touch. Human beings, no doubt, are charac-teristically good at ratiocination; but they are not to presume that thinking is better than feeling nor that argument is higher than activ-ity. Doing sums is no grander than building nests. It does not seem so clear to us as it did to St Thomas Aquinas that 'the contemplative life

[1] See p. 17 above

pursues man's proper course, namely the way of mind, whereas the active life is occupied with the interests we share with animals'.[2] It has come to seem questionable whether Reason is as excellent as our tradition has made it.

Once these difficulties have arisen, the question traditionally posed as 'What is man?' becomes harder to answer. It may be necessary to sit uncomfortably on a fence before finding a stable position. We have lost the confidence of Descartes that 'the difference that exists between men and brutes' is that people have minds and other creatures do not. His comparison of animals with machines, his conviction that animal dexterity is more like clockwork than intelligence, looks insensitive now. He sounds supercilious when he announces that the inability of non-human creatures to 'arrange words together ... does not merely show that the brutes have less reason than men, but that they have none at all, since it is clear that very little is required in order to talk'.[3]

Descartes has been pilloried for writing off animal life as merely mechanical. Now that we are more aware of the shocking cruelties which views like his may be used to justify, it might feel safer not to pursue this academic argument about the distinctiveness of human beings, but simply to express our disapproval and move on. To commend the rationality of human beings seems unsuitable, like repeating that Mussolini made the trains run on time. Just as we are not far enough away from Fascism as a frightening nightmare to weigh up neutrally any merits people might have seen in it, so most of us are not detached enough from the cruelties of factory farming to weigh up neutrally the ways in which people may be superior to animals.

There is scope for making more sensitive distinctions. Suppose that the tough notion that animals are merely automata is not only false in itself but also something of a caricature of Descartes' position. In an article in *Philosophy*,[4] John Cottingham argued that perhaps after all Descartes did not hold the 'monstrous view' that animals are 'totally without feeling'; and that there is 'even some positive evidence' that he held it false. Even if Descartes did believe that creatures without language cannot think and have no self-consciousness, this still leaves room for animals to have 'a level of feeling or sensation that falls short of reflective mental awareness'. So the enquiry about the status of animals may be pursued, even within

[2]   Aquinas, *Summa Theologica*, 1955
[3]   Descartes, *Discourse on Method*, 1637, Part V
[4]   Cottingham, 'A brute to the brutes? Descartes' treatment of animals', 1978

Descartes' terms of reference, without being committed in advance to insensitivity of our own. But Cottingham acknowledged, in fairness, that although Descartes' strict distinction between mind and body does not positively require the 'monstrous thesis' that animals have no feelings, it does at least make room for the belief that since they lack mind their bodies are not conscious at all. Cottingham's conclusion is that philosophy is seldom tidy. 'Descartes may not have been completely consistent, but at least he was not completely beastly to the beasts'.

Likewise Philip Devine, in a careful discussion of vegetarianism in the same number of *Philosophy*,[5] rejected the idea that animals are automata but proposed that animal pain might still count for less, being of lesser intensity than human pain. Some will be ready to consider his suggestion that animals 'experience far less suffering' as persuasive; advocates of animal rights will suspect special pleading. The argument about how animals may be treated goes on.

It is increasingly recognized that concern for animals is no fad. Vegetarianism is a stance which is increasingly respected. It does not therefore follow that human beings must be denied any special status. To treat 'man' as supreme remains a live option which plenty of responsible thinkers have continued to take for granted.

Gilbert Ryle, in a lecture published in 1962,[6] upheld the distinctiveness of human beings less bluntly than Descartes, by interpreting Reason more broadly. Not every human being need be a Thinker with a powerful intellect as distinct from an Agent; but it is still 'Thought that is peculiar to the human animal.' Rather than simply taking ratiocination as the sole ground of our uniqueness, he insisted that what is most distinctive about humanity is more fundamental than the ability to give reasons. What counts is 'using or misusing our wits'. Ryle described this sense of Thought as more 'hospitable', more open to a less narrow understanding.

Ryle's argument was wholly unrelated to the idea of the image of God; but he was no less sure than Christian contemporaries that human beings have possibilities for complex lives which are simply not open to lions. People 'may be or avoid being petty, impatient, and malicious'; or they may be fair-minded and calm; animals cannot. Of course Ryle was not making our capacity to be petty part of the glory of humanity. His point was that 'The only animal that is *either* irrational *or* rational is man.' Human beings know 'what it is

[5] Devine, 'The moral basis of vegetarianism', 1978
[6] Ryle, 'A rational animal', Auguste Comte Memorial Lecture, 1962

to get something wrong, and ... what it is to be in a muddle;' and not only know but care. In this sense of Thought he found their distinctive rationality.

Human beings who have pursued the argument about what humanity really is, and tried to understand their essential nature, have been happy and grateful to assume that *reason* must indeed be singled out as the defining characteristic of humankind. To call such gratitude misplaced would be ungenerous. Reason is indeed 'noble', even godlike. Our rationality is surely part of what it means to say that we are made in God's image.

This satisfaction needs to be qualified by the recognition that reason is too limited, or rather too specialized, to be the whole story. Thought, even in Ryle's broader sense, cannot be the sole basis of value. A more complete answer must take up, and go on from, the recognition that *minding* is a more important criterion for moral significance than intelligence. We mind about ourselves and one another. Our lives *matter* to us.[7] We have the ability to respond to what happens in the world, not only to think about it however rationally; and response is a value term.

The capacity to mind determines what ought to count as right or wrong ways to treat a conscious being. Our powers of reason are only part of our value in the eyes of our Creator. This sounds encouraging. There is more to us human beings than thinking. Christians can welcome Bentham's insistence that reason is not all that matters. They may not be so pleased with the corollary he promptly recognised, that human beings are not the only creatures with moral significance. 'The question is not, Can they reason? nor Can they talk? but Can they suffer?'

Many well-disposed people who warm to this still draw back from pursuing it in the direction of allowing animals full moral status. How far must we revise our behaviour to other living beings who evidently do not, in our sense, reason? As long as thinking and talking have been what counted, we have not been obliged to admit animals into our community. They are designated as 'dumb creatures', created for our sake. No doubt it is wrong to be cruel to them, but we have not felt compelled to worry about their rights.

Such pious certainty has begun to sound old-fashioned. Thoughtful Christians can no longer run away from the idea that the characteristics which make us matter morally are not all reserved to humanity. We are required to share our dignity with other creatures.

---

[7]   See Oppenheimer , 'Mattering', 1995

Suppose that after all the distinction between 'human' and 'animal' is not manifest enough to bear the moral weight we have put upon it. What happens then to 'man's dominion'? We do not want our ethical assumptions to become wobbly.

It would be wise not to hold on so defensively to the simple certainty that 'man' is the unique rational animal. We are not the only ones who care for our young, build homes, store up provisions, burrow in the earth, fly in the air, learn by experience, obey instructions, enjoy company. It should be possible to enquire about how human creatures can be compared with other animals without being thought to 'reduce' people to beasts.

To count ourselves as included in the whole creation among many fellow creatures could enlarge not shrink our understanding. We are part of a tremendous interlocking system. Whether we study or contemplate or simply relish the world of nature, it is fitting *both* to appreciate our own species as wonderful, *and* to go on to emphasize continuities well as discontinuities. The Great Chain of Being is an ancient way of looking at the natural creation, older than Darwin.[8] We should be glad to understand that the theory of evolution has given human beings a rightful, indeed a glorious, place in the chain.

The overwhelming scale of the natural creation, which science has opened up since Darwin, can magnify God without diminishing humanity. Human beings are more splendid, not less, for being part of this immensity. It stretches our minds to consider that our Maker, who can number the hairs of our heads, can number the stars of every galaxy. There are plenty of difficulties about faith in God, but the size of the creation need not be among them. People who believe that 'not a sparrow falls' without God's presence can add nowadays that not a dinosaur expired without the concern of its Creator.

St Paul doubted whether God cared for oxen.[9] Some people who are happy to look on large-scale creatures, wild or tame, as included in the loving regard of their Maker find themselves a good deal more doubtful about some of the small ones. Does God care for earwigs? J.B.S. Haldane, noting that there are fifty times as many kinds of beetle as kinds of mammal, commented wryly: 'The Creator, if He exists, has a special preference for beetles'.[10] To human beings, creepy-crawlies are not lovable. We seem programmed to shun some kinds of living being. Those of us who regard most insects as

[8]   Lovejoy, *The Great Chain of Being*, 1953
[9]   *I Corinthians* 1.9
[10] Haldane in a lecture given on 7th April 1951

part of the problem of evil can anyway take some encouragement from reminding ourselves that our seemingly irrational fear is not a wholly pointless vexation. It may have developed as an evolutionary benefit. Many insects are dangerous in ways which human beings are not unreasonable to try to avoid.

Though it is daunting to imagine spiders in the garden of Eden and woodlice in Noah's ark, we might learn to be reconciled with unwelcome fellow creatures. To repudiate them without more ado would be to stipulate a pettier universe, less spacious and less interesting than the one in which we find ourselves placed. Coleridge's Ancient Mariner found himself blessed when he saw the water-snakes as not repulsive but beautiful.

> Blue, glossy green and velvet black
> They coiled and swam, and every track
> Was a flash of golden fire.

By unobtrusively slipping in the serpentine 'coiled' alongside the handsome colours, he conveyed the paradox that repellent creatures can suddenly be seen as beautiful. 'That self-same moment I could pray.' Learning to look with appreciation at any wonderfully-made creature can be a rehearsal for worship. When God shows Job the magnificence of the natural creation, Job's surrender is appropriate not ignoble.[11]

The way creation is linked with glory and wonder can be brought out by contrast with the television programmes 'Walking with dinosaurs' [BBC 1, 1999]. The animals portrayed in these films, deduced from their bones and skilfully animated, were lifelike but not alive: full of interest, but not full of splendour. They could not elicit the kind of almost reverent attention which birdwatchers give to the natural world, which might even be called contemplation.

The series concentrated, not inaccurately but lopsidedly, on these animals as predators, on dramatic moments, on killing and being killed. There was no space to give an impression of the ordinariness of earthly life going on day after day, creatures subsisting and reproducing, flourishing or ailing, in times long before ours. These animated beasts were remarkable technical achievements, not fellow creatures inhabiting the earth.

Religious believers may worry that talk like this of 'fellow creatures' threatens to blur the line, once so easy to draw, between man and beast. People who find it uncongenial and even disturbing to

---

[11] 'I have heard of thee by the hearing of the ear: but now mine eye seeth thee. Wherefore I abhor myself, and repent in dust and ashes.' *Job* 42.5–6

think of human beings as bound in one bundle with the rest of creation will be inclined to take evasive action when the argument goes this way. They may laugh at anyone who tries to allow moral status to animals: she probably has a sentimental axe to grind about pets. Do grown-up people have to worry about whether there is a place in heaven for Fido? It is all very well to resort to mockery rather than look for answers; but the problem about how consideration for animals fits into Christian morality is not childish. The question can be put in a still more far-reaching form: How can human beings *and* animals fit into God's love for all creation?

Christian loyalty may not after all demand an absolute and sacrosanct distinction between human creatures and other animals. Christians believe that the *absolute* distinction is between divinity and humanity; yet the Almighty chooses to cross this divide, adopting human creatures as honorary sons and daughters of God.[12] It would be a less surprising, and congruous, step to imagine that human beings in turn may blur the *relative* distinction between people and animals, and let animals come in as honorary persons. People include animals in their households and undertake responsibility for them, adopting them as almost literally family members. If 'pets' seems patronizing, they are 'companion animals'.[13] One may consider this kind of human grace as a true small-scale picture of what divine grace is like. Many children and many adults would be happy to think in this way.

The picture is only an analogy and so far leaves wild animals outside our moral concern as not persons at all. Perhaps the ethical significance of most of the natural creation is not for us to determine, even benignly. Yet surely it cannot be only the domestic animals whose biographies are entwined with ours who matter for their own sakes and who have moral status in the eyes of their Maker. Unless we mean to go back before Darwin and reject evolution, we are obliged, not merely allowed, to recognize that there can be no sharp factual, or moral, cut-off point between ourselves and all the other animals. We can understand, some of us with relish, that human mattering cannot be unique, once we realise that human beings developed gradually from ancestors who could not be classified as human.

To accept that *homo* is descended from *austrolopithecus*[14] implies that there is a historical story to be told about our origins, however

[12] *Galatians* 4.4–5
[13] Sharpe, 2005
[14] Agreeably explained in Johanson and Edey, *Lucy:* 1981

long ago we believe that human beings began. What still worries Christians about this story is its implication that creatures without souls suddenly became the parents of creatures with souls. People who are convinced that human beings are special among animals, because they alone are made in the image of God, seem to be committed to maintain a fine but plain distinction at some point in our evolution, dividing an animal parent from a human child. When this is spelt out it can look decidedly implausible. It is all very well for an unpretentious woman to be amazed to realise that she is bringing up a genius; but this would just be a difference of degree. A mother ape cherishing a baby who counts as human would represent, precisely, a difference of kind. Would St Peter keep the heavenly gates shut in the face of a new arrival, saying, 'I can't let this one in: he's a missing link'? It is only too natural, if lines are to be drawn, to set about drawing them legalistically.

Paul Badham, in *Immortality or Extinction?*, admitted and emphasized the absence of a clear line between human beings and animals, and identified this as a major problem for believers in eternal life. He suspected that the primary reason why the intelligent 'Australopithecine cousins' of *homo habilis* are left on the wrong side of the line, having failed to qualify as human, is not that they failed to meet the necessary criteria but merely that they happened to become extinct. None the less he still maintained that 'the line has to be drawn somewhere if man is held to enjoy an eternal destiny which apes are denied.' He was faced by the problem that one generation at the boundary must have 'passed into oblivion, while the next generation were sufficiently man-like to be heirs of eternal life.' What, he had to ask, 'would the children think of this? Would they know that their parents were 'only animals', while they themselves were a new kind of being?'[15]

It is the supposedly sharp cut-off point between human beings and animals which creates such difficulties. It is not unsound to draw blurred lines when reality is blurred. If Christians are not committed to a quasi-legal frontier, they need be no more dismayed than anyone else by problems about which candidates are to be counted in and which out. On the contrary, unless they are called to legislate or to set examinations, they can afford to allow boundaries to be vague.

It appears that the boundary line between species really has turned out to be fuzzy. This is the familiar practical difficulty of the borderline case. A boy has to be considered too young to marry one

[15] Badham, *Immortality or Extinction?*, 1982, p. 47

day, and old enough the next because it happens to be his sixteenth birthday. We still have a useful concept of maturity, perplexing as it may sometimes be to apply. An embryo becomes a fetus and then a baby, somewhere on the way between conception and birth, neither of which itself is a simple distinct moment. It may be hard to say whether this tint is red or orange, but we are not thrown into confusion about whether one can distinguish colours at all.

It is not as theologically worrying as it sounds to announce that there must have been animals, in historical reality, whose offspring could have been classified as human. Badham refers politely to the argument about drawing or not drawing lines which Austin Farrer applied to disabled human beings, 'that God will love and save whatever is there to be loved and saved, and that God will make no arbitrary discriminations.' Farrer refused to 'attribute to God the mentality of a government clerk, who would rather distribute no benefits at all, than lack a clear rule of thumb by which to assign them.' Instead of building on this Badham moves back into legalism: 'even God must draw the line somewhere'. Is this really so? Is drawing lines the right analogy at all?[16]

The idea that boundaries may be, and often are, *fuzzy* has more to be said for it than impatient legislators may suppose. Resistance to a demand for sharp distinctions is relevant also to Regan's all-or-nothing case for animal rights (see above, p. 19). He insists on a cut-off point: a creature either simply has 'inherent value', in his sense, or it simply does not: 'There are no in-betweens. Moreover, all those who have it, have it equally. It does not come in degrees.' This sounds splendid until one tries to apply it. It seems profoundly legalistic to imagine a click! when 'normal mammalian animals, aged one or more' suddenly qualify as bearers of rights. The notion that animals have 'inherent value' which gives them real moral status might be less neglected if people did not feel obliged to define it so strictly.

Likewise it may be replied to Badham that it would be good to have a rest from making rules about what shall count as a sacred soul and what shall not. Any living being is precious to its Maker in whatever ways it may turn out to be capable of receiving God's love. Surely God can be trusted to do appropriate justice to all manner of creatures.

It is capacity to receive love that makes a human being or an animal a candidate, so to speak, for eternal life. Some minimum *capacity*

---

[16] Badham, 1982, p. 46 and Farrer, *Love Almighty and Ills Unlimited*, 1966, p. 190

for response[17] is indeed the sign. Responding is more than reacting to a stimulus. To suggest that any creature might 'have a soul' is at least to say that he, she or it is able to take heed of what happens and in some degree to mind about itself and other creatures. A gorilla cares for her offspring in a sense in which an earwig after all can not.

Rather than insisting that a creature must either have an immortal soul, or lack one, we can understand what 'soul' means in a way which allows more flexibility. Suppose that a soul is not a *thing*, detachable from its body and maybe imperishable, but is better described as a *pattern*. People who believe in a God of love who made all manner of creatures may think of souls as, so to speak, patterns of lovability.[18] This is where the value, and indeed the sacredness, of a life is located.

For Christian believers resurrection, by grace, of a life valued by God is a more convincing alternative to extinction than the natural immortality of a separate part of us called a soul.[19] Death is real and people and animals die, but the pattern of some individual creatures' lives will not be permanently extinguished. Their Creator is able to restore them to new vitality. A good analogy is the hardware and the software of a computer.[20] If the hardware of my computer is at its last gasp, all the material which has been saved should be capable of being transferred without loss to a new and one hopes improved model.

---

[17] Oppenheimer, *Looking Before and After*, 1988, p. 83
[18] I first looked at the idea of the soul as a pattern in a sermon I preached in the University of Oxford, February 1979, which was printed in *Theology*, September 1979 as 'Life after death'. I expanded these notions further in *The Hope of Happiness*, 1983; in *Looking Before and After*; and in 'Ourselves, our souls and bodies', 1991.
[19] Oppenheimer, 1988, ch. 7 and see below in Chapter 9, p. 71
[20] Oppenheimer, 1988, p. 85

Chapter 5

Responding

He that hath an ear, let him hear what the Spirit saith unto the churches; To him that overcometh will I give … a white stone, and in the stone a new name written, which no man knoweth save him that receiveth it.

Revelation 2.17

Human beings ought to be celebrated, and can be celebrated, without belittling any other creature. Appreciation of humanity need not be side-tracked by constant comparisons, unfavourable or even favourable, with other animals. We do not have to think about the whole creation all the time. If we are happy to be human, we may be allowed to have a kind of patriotism for our own species. We can call ourselves 'humanist' without implications of disbelief in God or arrogance towards animals.

People who take heed of human excellence need not always be haunted by the disagreeable word 'speciesist'. Delighting in human wit and wisdom is as innocent as delighting in the beauty of butterflies. To belittle the 'capability and god-like reason' of humankind is not the virtue of humility but the vice of ingratitude.

We should be able to celebrate our own gifts without having to be possessive about them. There is no need to feel anxious when we find ourselves sharing the characteristic excellences of human beings with other animals. The glory of humanity is not such a tender plant that it needs to be surrounded by a fence to keep other creatures outside. The privilege of being a child of God is more like belonging to an extended family than belonging to an exclusive club. The likenesses and differences between creatures need not be entered into a competition. Making comparisons ought to be a positive activity, exploring the characteristics of variegated animals in the hope of shedding reciprocal light.

What are the particular attributes of human beings, which allow us to say that they are made in God's own image? Reason indeed is

godlike, but the foundation has already been laid for not setting reason on a lonely height. To emphasize as more fundamental the
capacity to *respond*, to mind about ourselves and one another, allows
human excellences to be put in context. Whatever turns out to be distinctively valuable about us is rooted in our responsiveness as conscious beings.

Consciousness is a philosophers' mystery, but it is not compulsory
to understand it before being able to take it into account. Commonsense can anyway affirm that some bodies undeniably are conscious,
without having to start by answering the ancient question of what
consciousness is and how people's minds are related to their bodies.
There are certainly beings in the universe who in various degrees are
aware of their surroundings. They respond in simple or complex
ways, passively or actively, to what is going on around them. They
take more or less notice of one another. The notion of a *self* begins to
apply: that is, an individual who has experiences, a subject who is
not only an object.

There is a further stage which is particularly characteristic of
human beings. People are not just conscious in the way we think
dogs are conscious. People not only have experiences, agreeable or
disagreeable: they know that they are having experiences. Self-conscious beings can take heed of what they themselves are, what it is
like to be them. The plainest mark of self-consciousness is language.
Putting experience into words makes it possible to go beyond a simple awareness of what is happening and to realise that it is happening to *me*. We can certainly call this, if we like, the dawn of reason.

There is still no need to draw a sharp line. Rather than hunting for
any distinct cut-off point, we can follow a progression of increasing
awareness, from lifeless material objects, to living creatures, to individuals with feelings, to social animals, to people. William Wordsworth included plants in the company of beings who are not just
alive but responsive:

'Tis my faith that every flower
Enjoys the air it breathes.[1]

Seriously as he made this announcement, on the whole we treat it as
a flight of poetic imagination. People who are said to talk to trees
tend to be laughed at. It is not sensible in plain prose to imagine that
plants are conscious, let alone self-conscious. There is no answer to

[1]   Wordsworth, 'Lines written in early spring'

the question what it would be like to be a daffodil; though philosophers have raised the question what it would be like to be a bat.[2]

Flowers and bats, as well as many simpler creatures such as bacte-
ria and amoebae, are not inert material objects like pebbles but creatures with lives. They have more in common with rooks than they
have with rocks. We do not need to think of slugs and snails as conscious to describe them as flourishing or languishing. To call them
alive is to believe that there are answers to questions about what is
good for them. Living creatures can be damaged even if we do not
think they can be hurt.

Consciousness is a stage beyond simply being alive. Once creatures have reached this level and awareness has dawned, it becomes
natural to suppose that now they really are capable of enjoying the
air they breathe. It seems to make sense to say that a sparrow or a lion
experiences the world as a better or a worse place. It not only flour-
ishes but in some simple way *wants* to flourish. It is *in its interest* to be
in good health. We may say something further. We can suppose,
without any metaphor, that a live animal has *intentions*, whether elementary and instinctive or sophisticated and purposeful. Mammals
and birds, at least, can try to do things: to gather food, to escape danger, to attract a mate.

All this can be summed up, not too fancifully, by saying that
whereas living creatures can flourish, conscious creatures can *mind*.
When minding begins, values come in.[3] Though we do not have to
go so far as to say that animals 'have minds', there should be no
denying that they can experience pleasure and pain. Whether something or someone has enough awareness to care about what happens
can hardly be morally insignificant. It matters, at least a little, what
creatures want and whether they get it. This is what Bentham
meant by insisting on the question, 'Can they suffer?' Values have a
foothold in minding. A world with conscious creatures in it is a world
in which the notions of 'good' and 'bad' apply.

Believers in God are apt to say that the values which are there to be
minded about, goodness, truth and beauty, are made by God. It is
more accurate to suppose that what God creates directly is a world of
facts. God's command is not, 'Let there be beauty', but 'Let there be
light'; and light is beautiful. It gives creatures the kind of experience

[2]   T. Nagel, 'What is it like to be a bat?', 1979
[3]   Oppenheimer, 1995, p. 63

that they want to have. The creation of facts gives rise to real values, because facts soon turn out to be, not value-free, but value-laden.[4]

If we had to suppose that God ordained values, we should have to imagine God saying, 'I have decided that killing shall be wrong.' In that case, to be killed might have been beneficial, except that God has decreed otherwise. It makes more sense to say that God creates a universe inhabited by active conscious creatures who can do one another good and harm. Conscious creatures have purposes and values emerge from the fulfilment or frustration of purposes.

To ask, 'What do I want?' is a question of fact. To ask, 'Is this worth wanting?' or 'What ought I to do about it in the light of what other people want?' are questions of value. When Cain has killed Abel, on purpose, the fact is that Abel is dead. But his death is not a value-free fact. Cain has done Abel objective harm by putting an end to the fulfilment of all Abel's purposes. That is why Cain's act is not neutral nor good but evil, and Abel's blood cries out to God in protest. Murder is the sort of killing which has wrongness built into it, because people mind being killed.

The created universe as a whole is not value-free, but must turn out in the end to be either worthwhile or not, to its Maker and to its occupants. An individual action, a killing or a rescuing, may be simply bad or good, but the worthwhileness of the whole universe can hardly be a plain Yes or No. Purposes can and do conflict, so we cannot expect questions about what really is worthwhile to be simple. The complexity of values is the complexity of ethics. Answers to questions about ethics are a matter of whether purposes can be harmonized.

As soon as believers announce that God's creation really is worthwhile, the problem of evil is standing in the wings ready to make its entrance when something goes wrong. If it turned out at last that human beings are not of lasting value after all and that their excellences are of no ultimate account, or that their purposes cannot be harmonized and their wants satisfied, then 'God saw that it was good' could not be said, and faith would be refuted.

There is one basic reply which Christians must make when the sufferings of the world threaten to destroy faith, that the God they believe in has the right to call creation good, because the Creator is not a remote Deity beyond the starry sky, untouched by pain, pronouncing from on high that it is all worth while, or still more harshly that our troubles are all our own fault. Sin accounts for a great deal of

[4]   Oppenheimer, 'Ought and is', 1965, p. 11

evil, but not enough to make the universe fair. The creation with all its sufferings is God's responsibility; and the God who is Father, Son and Holy Spirit accepts the responsibility. If there is to be blame, God takes the blame.[5]

That is an essential start. There must be more to be said, because evil, as people experience it, is not simply a sort of generalized sickness of all things earthly, curable by one decisive treatment. People suffer individually from specific afflictions which they find themselves having to bear for themselves. The question that suffering poses is whether the responsiveness which gives us our value brings with it too high a price in diverse particular pains and sorrows to allow honest people to believe in a good God who allowed all this. Once concern about the troubles of God's children takes hold, how can thoughtful believers not make this their primary concern? For the second time, and still more comprehensively than the matter of animal rights, an urgent ethical difficulty seems to have pushed its way in, demanding resolution and making consideration of human value and attention to human glory look like a tempting distraction.

Must everything else be put aside in order to face the demand to 'justify the ways of God to man'?[6] Imperative though it is to be aware, continually aware, of the groaning and travailing of creation, it is still not compulsory to abandon every other project until the problem of evil can be solved. On the contrary, the longest way round may turn out to be, not just a permissible route, but the shortest way home. Rushing to defend the faith directly in the face of this or that intractable difficulty seldom succeeds in satisfying doubters who want an answer to human troubles. Arguments that people's afflictions are really for the best are generally inadequate and sometimes insulting. An exploration which sets off, like Alice, in a contrary direction may be more promising. The enterprise of considering, in the light of Christian faith, what positive account can be given of human significance and human hopes is not only a worthwhile endeavour for its own sake, but may help to loosen the grip of the problem of evil by allowing the mixed woe and delight of creation to seem less pointless.

The pervasiveness of evil is a fact, neither to be ignored nor to be made the whole story of human life. People are often unable to give an answer on demand to the enquiry, 'How can this outcome, this assemblage of facts, be called good?' What is required of faith is nei-

[5]   Oppenheimer, 2001; also see below, p. 115
[6]   Milton, *Paradise Lost*, Book 1

ther to give up in despair nor to settle for a hasty and heartless answer. The pious recommendation that simple trust is the answer is all very well, but people who have already got beyond simplicity cannot produce trust to order, certainly not by closing their minds and disregarding the apparent facts. Even if they can quieten their own doubts that way, they will be a hindrance rather than a help to one another. Credulity may be touching; but the virtue of faith is better described in terms of the loyalty which takes a firm grasp of what has become clear so far and then keeps on trying to see what can be built on it. Christians who find that belief is hard are not therefore unfaithful. They can be grateful to take St Thomas as a patron saint. He was not blamed for his honest doubt but on the contrary he was granted the assurance he had demanded.

Believers who are prepared to face their doubts may expect to start by proving the existence of God and then to go on to construct whatever they want to say about God's creation on that basis. Too often the proposed proofs look like rabbits planted in agnostic hats by sleight of hand, ready to emerge triumphantly, clever not conclusive. Today an enquiring believer who cannot be satisfied without evidence may be encouraged to proceed in the way a scientist proceeds. Strange and even shocking as it may sound, the assertions of faith present themselves as hypotheses in search of confirmation.[7] Putting ideas about God to the test is not putting God to the test. The calling of some Christians is the positive and fundamentally loyal activity of exploring the meaning of theological statements and trying to find out whether in the long run they can stand up.

To see whether the whole Christian story does or does not carry conviction, it is thoroughly promising to consider seriously what account it has to offer of human beings and their place in the universe. There is a less obvious analogy than starting at ground level for the way faith can be firmly founded. The keystone of an arch which holds it up is laid at the end of the work, and meanwhile temporary shuttering keep the building from falling. It is a paradoxical but congenial notion that likewise Christian belief may be imagined as bound together from above.

---

[7]   See Preface, p. 1 above

Chapter 6
Loving

My weight is my love ...

Augustine, Confessions, XIII. 9

The responsible hypothesis which is in search of confirmation is that human beings are creatures, made 'in the image of God'. *Suppose* this is true. What does it mean and does the whole story make sense? The kind of sense it needs to make is not a piece of deduction that ends in 'QED', but the encouragement which experience offers that having come so far it is worth going on. Believers bear witness to a common-sense kind of long-term verification[1] that their faith holds good, in the kind of way that people's faith in one another holds good.

Rather than demanding proof at the beginning *or else*, at least it is worth setting out with believers on the way they are following to see where it arrives. Of course there is always wishful thinking to take travellers off the track, but it is not only religious people who wishfully think. Some people would rather not be bothered by religion and are content to ignore its claims and stay put rather than explore. They counterbalance the people who take a stand on pious assumptions which they dare not doubt. Both sets of people may be challenged to argue their conclusions before settling down in the most comfortable position.

For people who are willing to move forward, hoping to make discoveries, the Christian path may lead straight into the tangle of sceptical brambles which is the problem of evil, still blocking the way. The argument so far has been that the sensible course is to break through the brambles as best one can, without stopping to uproot them all before gong any further. The motive for pushing on is not to relax forthwith in green pastures, but to have the chance to explore the promising territory of humanity and what it is to be a human creature. The humanist hope of understanding ourselves better is

---

[1] Basil Mitchell discusses the nature of a cumulative case in *The Justification of Religious Belief*, 1973.

worthwhile in itself; and the larger prospect opens up of making more sense of what believers say about their Maker.

At the beginning of the exploration it needs to be reiterated that it is an exploration not an invasion. We have no right to claim sole possession, on behalf of humanity, of all the riches the territory around us offers. We find ourselves among innumerable fellow creatures who are not to be belittled nor forgotten. Convinced as we may be that humankind is the species which is made in the image of God, we are still not called upon to take our singular excellence for granted. It is more illuminating to think about 'characteristic' human endowments than 'unique' human endowments. Rather than placing human glory in competitive opposition to the grandeur of all the works of the Lord, it is more seemly to praise our Maker more comprehensively, counting ourselves as part of the Great Chain of Being (see above p. 33).

What is it about human beings that is supposed to make them god-like? The favourite candidate, reason, has been respectfully set aside as anyway not the only answer, and the way is clear now to take up and build upon the thought of *responsiveness* as the foundation of God's image in humanity. 'Responding', 'minding' and 'loving' are not synonyms, but their meanings are related and interdependent. To mind about what happens and to have the capacity to respond to it provide the necessary basis for being a creature who can love, made in the 'image and likeness' of the God who is said to be Love personified.

So the Christian emphasis on love comes into full view. A short look at a concordance exhibits how pervasive throughout the whole New Testament is 'love' as a keyword: the love of God, the love of Christ, love as the great commandment, love as the new Christian commandment, love for one another, love for enemies. The theme is so fundamental in the Christian Gospel that any Christian who is trying to give an account of what human beings really are could almost leave out the centrality of love as too obvious to mention.

When we are trying to identify the character of human nature, comparing but especially contrasting ourselves with the other animals, we find a host of miscellaneous qualifications. We think, we talk, we pray, we walk upright and use our hands for gripping,[2] we not only use but manufacture tools, we control fire and cook our

---

[2]   For the human 'precision grip', see e.g. Leakey, *Human Origins*, 1982, p. 10. For bipedalism and its importance, see Johanson & Edey, 1981.

food,[3] we create works of art, we laugh, we cry, we organize. Rather than plunging straight into the details, we may hope to avoid getting lost by first doing some organizing. We can pick out one heading which identifies better than any of these particular skills the distinctiveness of humanity. Without belittling the grandeur of rationality, it appears that to nominate 'love' as the mainspring of human living is the most promising way of identifying what it can mean to be made in God's image.

A high-minded, but false, next step is duly to assign love the place of honour but to reduce its meaning to a well-meaning cliché. To love, no doubt, is to wish somebody's good, not to want anything for oneself. Christians even take credit for recognizing nothing as authentic love except an attitude of impersonal benevolence.[4] So they lose sight of the truth that love whether divine or human cannot be so indifferent.[5] In order to signify anything in particular, love must function as a driving force. What people love, they put their hearts into. The element of *minding* is essential. To leave this emphasis out of the Christian faith as if it were somehow unworthy would be to forsake the Bible. There is nothing impersonal about the God of Abraham, Isaac and Jacob. People are like the God who made them because they are not impersonally neutral about the world. They want things and they care about their own and other people's lives.

Another temptation for Christians is to identify the love of God entirely with the love of the Redeemer, by-passing the love of the Creator, forgetting that making came before saving. 'And God saw everything that he had made, and behold, it was very good,' indicates that the universe came into being because God wanted it. Thomas Traherne expressed this magnificently:

> It is very strange; Want itself is a Treasure in heaven ... But the LORD GOD of Israel the living and true God, was from all Eternity, and from all Eternity wanted like a GOD. He wanted the Communication of his Divine Essence, and Persons to Enjoy it. He wanted Worlds, He wanted Spectators, He wanted Joys, He wanted Treasures. He wanted, yet he wanted not, for He had them.[6]

A snag about taking 'love' as the keyword which sums up this whole line of thought is that even more than most important words it lends itself to some vague and hazy ways of speaking. It sinks into

[3]   See Leakey & Lewin, 1977, pp. 139–40; see also below, p. 65
[4]   Nygren, *Agape and Eros*, 1969
[5]   Oppenheimer, 1983
[6]   Traherne, *Centuries* I , 41, 1958

sentimentality and is used as a kind of woolly blanket to wrap up indeterminate comfort. If *capacity to love* is indeed to be a profitable way of identifying what matters most about human beings, it must be characterized more definitely: first by what it is not, then by what it is. The negative route can turn out to have a affirmative upshot, like Alice's walk in the contrary direction. Instead of commending love by offering positive but vague praise of the human ideals we hope to realise, to begin instead by repudiating what is apt to go wrong, what is incompatible with love, can be a short cut to finding a distinctive notion of humanity.

People should be loving: but what should they not be? To call people *in*human, bad examples of humanity, has an ordinary meaning which shows by direct contrast the main criterion for qualifying as an acceptable human being. To call people 'inhuman' is to call them hardhearted and unresponsive. People who are stupid and irrational may be found exasperating, but not inhuman. When we are making judgments of value, the 'rational animal' looks a little like a red herring. What we have in common is 'one human heart', said Wordsworth.[7] From this direction it is plain to see that it is our minding, responsiveness, love, not only our brainpower, which are the characteristic aspects of humanity which illuminate best the particular significance of our species.

Whatever keyword we take, it is not for obliterating the details but for arranging them. A theology of human beings should be glad to recognize what it is about humanity that has made us worth creating, and then worth saving when things went wrong. Christian thinkers may and should pursue this enterprise of making sense of our value to ourselves, to one another and to our Creator. There is plenty of scope for attending to the distinctive qualities of human beings, as well as for making comparisons and contrasts with other creatures.

Some Christians will still be inclined to insist that the whole enquiry into what makes humanity worthwhile is suspect. The question why God loves us is supposed to have one simple answer which rules out any recognition of human excellence. We have been instructed to believe that God's love for us has nothing to do with what we are like but comes wholly from God's own nature. It is a mystery which we can never deserve or explain, for which we can only give back our thankful praise. To add anything to that basis must seem simply presumptuous; but still there is something essen-

---

[7] Wordsworth, 'The old Cumberland Beggar'

tial to be said. For all the damage done by sin, in the beginning 'God saw that it was good'. It does no honour to God to suppose that his creatures are worthless. Believing that there was some point in bringing human beings into existence is more reverent than to imagine a divine artist doodling, or worse still bungling and then putting things right as a sort of afterthought. To be humanist enough to affirm that God's creatures are endowed with some real value is not just a tenacious error. To investigate what that value connotes is a valid vocation. Of course we are not to claim merit: 'It is he that hath made us and not we ourselves.' On this basis, that we should think of ourselves as God's artefacts, we may and should dare to acknowledge glory.

The case for allowing humanism into faith becomes stronger not weaker when we move from creating to saving. Believers can enter into their heritage when they realise that they are not only the handiwork of an artist but people who are chosen and wanted. In the Christian tradition human beings are the adopted children of God. It would be positively ungrateful not to suppose that they are valuable for themselves in the way that beloved children are valuable for themselves. The question, *Why* does God love us? may not make sense, but it does make sense to ask, *What* are these creatures like that God loves? What does make human beings special? Believers are not straying when they set about exploring the territory of humanity and what it is to be a human creature.

There are many characteristic excellencies of human beings. To set about ranking them in order of merit would be a temptation rather than a help, especially as they all depend upon each other. The one necessary basis on which everything else depends has already been identified. There could be no excellence if there were no such thing as conscious experience, which is aware of better and worse and which fills the world with values by minding about better and worse. It does not follow that responsiveness is the most excellent excellence. Foundations are the most essential part of a house but it would be nonsense to nominate them as the best.

The foundation is not quite laid yet. A creature alone in its world could be responsive. It could react to its experience, suffer or be pleased; but it takes more than this to make a human life. A normal reaction to the idea of such a limited existence is horror. Solitary confinement is one of the worst punishments we can imagine. In the world we are living in, responsiveness is reciprocal. Human beings, and maybe some animals, not only mind what happens to themselves, they mind about one another. It is this *mutual* minding which is the central meaning of love.

For creatures who have self-awareness, the two-way character of responsiveness is the foundation of morality. Values are built into facts because *I* am not the only one who matters. People have duties because other people mind what they do. Then, beyond the ethic of duty, the ethic of generosity comes into play, the kindness which makes life worth living by going beyond what is strictly compulsory. All this is the background to the whole picture of human nature and the particular characteristics of human beings which make them worthwhile creatures: still without prejudice to the worthwhileness of any other creature.

Chapter 7

Recognizing

That our sons shall grow up as the young plants:
   and that our daughters shall be as the polished corners
   of the temple.

Psalm 144.12

Beyond responsiveness there is self-awareness and self-awareness arrives with awareness of each other. We can tell each other apart and there is more in this truism than might appear. The capacity for living our lives in relationship to one another is a basic human excellence. This means more than our inclination to want company, as flock animals presumably do. It means, in the positive sense, discriminating: distinguishing individuals from each another as a foundation for social life.[1]

Once again, singling out the recognition of other people as a special human aptitude is a matter of 'compare and contrast'. Human beings have no monopoly of this advantage, although it may be tempting to think so. Many animals can recognize one another and individual human beings, and some can respond to the names they have been given. There is still a central difference. What does not appear, even among the apes our near relatives, is the capacity to name one another.

Does this practical and intellectual skill of ours carry with it greater moral importance? The argument about 'speciesism' is still very much alive. Defending experiments on animals, John W. Funder insisted upon giving 'individual' a stronger meaning for human beings than for other animals. He declared himself to be 'in awe and wonder at particular human individuals (family members, Mozart, etc.), but not individual rats.' This 'absolute distinction in ethical terms', he explained, 'is based on intuition, and supported by arguments which I find convincing; others, perhaps, find them less so'.[2]

---

[1]   See above, p. 17
[2]   Funder,1989, pp. 17, 14

Others do indeed 'find them less so' and argue that people should not assume the right to use other sentient creatures for human ends. Some look upon even kindly notions of human superiority as deeply patronizing to our fellow creatures. There is a huge and recalcitrant argument here about human attitudes to the domestic animals whom we name and teach to recognize us. For many human beings, their affection for individual animals is of profound importance; but others would even deny any merit to these rewarding relationships, because although people love their pets and care for them they do not acknowledge them as rights-bearers.

Is keeping a dog a form of self-indulgence? Peter Singer determinedly puts the phrase 'animal lover' in scornful inverted commas in the name of justice. Lynne Sharpe turns the argument round with refreshing common sense. She comments that it is Singer who 'fails to see animals as *individuals*'. The point of 'companion animals' is not the service we require from them but 'the relationship which makes it possible.' 'People live with dogs because they get on well with dogs.'[3]

There will hardly be a conclusive resolution of these diverse stances. Lynne Sharpe's discussion is about animals tamed by people. She stops short of asking how to think ethically about the lives of wild creatures, some of whom are surely individuals but who are not and cannot be members of human communities. The 'real social relationships' with 'partner animals' which are her theme are based on trust; and though we may teach a chimpanzee to use words 'we cannot trust him' (p. 108).

In an interesting article called 'Dogs and slaves', D.H.M. Brooks goes behind the question of the ethics of pet-keeping to the question of whether the way people have *bred* dogs has been a kind of exploitation, in the same sort of way as breeding human beings as slaves would be exploitation. If so, to urge the contented affection of individual slaves or animals, or the trustful relationships people can have with them, would not in either case be an adequate answer. He puts the case sternly, suggesting that we may have 'systematically distorted the psyche of another species for our own emotional gratification'.[4] Upholders of animal rights will warm to this and may readily believe that 'we' did it on purpose.

Brooks' own conclusion is more subtle: 'A good situation may come about by questionable means' (p. 37). Both human beings and

[3]   Sharpe, 2005, pp. 77–8
[4]   Brooks, 'Dogs and slaves', 1987–8, p. 35

dogs benefit greatly from their association. This is not the facile defence of the slave-owner, 'My slaves are well treated.' It is rather that dogs have evolved, have admittedly been caused to evolve by their dealings with human beings, into a domesticated species. Their condition is different from the situation of enslaved people. If dogs were set free, they could not return to being wolves. They truly are better off as they are. The individuals are not exploited; and does it make any sense to exploit a species? (pp. 55–6).

When the argument moves on from the ethics of breeding dogs to the, so far imaginary, case of breeding human beings as genetic slaves, moral wrongness emerges more plainly. Brooks is so well aware of the ethical complexity of what makes a life worthwhile that eventually he sits on the fence. He does not know what 'directions should be followed if we are given the power to change ourselves and produce another kind of being?' (p. 64).

Religious believers may hope that biblical teaching will offer them authoritative guidance, but anyone who approaches the moral questions about the taming of animals from a Darwinian direction will not find much help in the scriptures. Scientists, whether Christian or not, have to look at the story of how humankind has impinged upon the natural world with neutral detachment. They cannot bring in the idea that the human role in that story could have been a divinely delegated responsibility. The theological notion that human care for animals could be analogous to divine grace may seem irrelevantly whimsical.[5]

Yet Christians can still find it worthwhile to apply the ethics and the theology to one another. The story of benign human care for another species, in order to enter into quasi-personal relationships with individuals, bears comparison with the story that human beings are created in order to enter individually into the love of God. The attitude of dogs to their masters has often been characterized, approvingly or otherwise, as worship.

For anybody who is seized by the idea of animal rights, this will never do. This whole attitude to animals is bound to look oppressive. The doctrine that human beings have a special position because they are made in the divine image will appear more unfair than ever. Why should some of God's creatures have grander prospects than others? For people in the Jewish and Christian tradition, the question has a relevant familiarity. The idea that humanity has after all a special vocation among God's creatures is consonant with the ancient belief that one people has a distinct vocation among human

---

[5]   See above, p. 35

beings, not a moral superiority but an appointed role. If either of these ideas makes sense, the other may as well.

The concept of vocation has been obscured and made difficult to understand by the Fall. Neither the chosen people nor humanity have lived up to their high position. 'This is my vocation' is too likely to be an excuse for self-indulgence for myself and unkindness for everyone else. 'Calling' is a near-synonym which may be more useful, being both more humble and more business-like. Callings may be grand or modest, from the conversion of St Paul to the job-seeking of a school-leaver; but the point of a calling is to be a summons, not just an option. Callings to live in a particular way are mandatory, not made up. If arrogance comes in, it is an aberration.

If Christians can safely traverse the minefield of 'speciesism', they should be at ease with the idea that people and animals are all creatures of God. They may emphasize, not be embarrassed, by the fact that human excellences in general have evolved from our animal heritage. To look at both contrasts and comparison with other creatures offers a good prospect of understanding the gifts of human creatures better. The particular excellence which is the capacity to recognize other individuals is far from being merely an agreeable accomplishment which happens to be characteristic of people. Many other creatures have this ability in varying degrees and its biological benefit is evident. Much follows from it.

A major and basic manifestation of this capacity to identify one another is the way in which human animals reproduce their species. They find mates and they rear families, taking care of their own babies and children, nourishing, protecting and educating them so that they can grow slowly to complex and variegated maturity.

Human beings have evolved further than other animals in the extent to which they not only recognize their children as their own but distinguish them one from another. They relate to them not just as progeny but as the individuals they are, loving them 'all alike' indeed but in another sense loving them all differently. Welcoming babies with naming rites is characteristic of human societies. When human young 'leave the nest' their parents remain recognizably parents, deeply concerned for their children long after they have ceased to be children. It has been suggested that the seemingly pointless prolongation of the human lifespan, long after women's child-bearing years, has an evolutionary function. Grandparents have a role in the extended family which is good for the survival of new generations.

This evident difference from the profound but temporary parental attachments characteristic of other kinds of creature can still be a difference of degree not a difference of kind. Far from being a human monopoly, the love that human beings have for their progeny, of all loves, has deep roots in our animal ancestry. There are many kinds of animal for whom to 'be fruitful and multiply' means, not only to bring offspring to birth, but to go on to bring them *up*, before sending them out into the world. Parental devotion, whatever more it may become, is an animal trait, especially characteristic of birds and mammals. It is no less excellent for its primitive origins. There is no need to claim uniqueness in order to acknowledge glory.

It is this love of one's own children, however modest its origins, which has the distinction of being the authorized Christian analogy for the love of God. Christians call God Father, and sometimes argue about whether they might also call God Mother, surely knowing full well that this is not literal but figurative language. It is by being an image of the grace of God, not in its own right, that even the most devoted human care can be characterized as godlike.

There is no need to think that if only we could repudiate our descent from the beasts we could strengthen the analogy and put the comparison of human parental love to God's love on a more divine and less presumptuous footing. On the contrary, it is worth remembering the less-than-dignified metaphor of a mother hen gathering her chickens under her wing, which the Lord used as a picture of God's own care. It must be more reverent to speak about God with the help of variegated analogies which we could not possibly claim to be adequate, than to suppose that God's transcendence could be captured with one dominant image. The assurance of the Psalmist, 'Thou shalt be safe under his feathers' is not really more audacious than confidence in God's victory 'with his own right hand and with his holy arm'. Indeed, the authoritative comparison of God's Spirit with a brooding dove might be a corrective to the human presumption that our creation in God's image and likeness makes us incomparably grander than the fowls of the air.

If one is particularly anxious to identify the uniqueness of human beings, the love of parents for their offspring is not the place to look. The enterprise of exploring what makes humanity special can be taken further. The characteristic minding and mattering of human beings which makes them loving and lovable can be illuminated by contrast as well as by comparison, moving on from the instinctive attachments of animals towards the kinds of human love which are more voluntary and have more to do with our self-consciousness.

The attraction between a man and a woman which produces human offspring has developed further from its animal origins than the love of a mother for her infant. Mary Midgley pleasingly characterized the meaning of sex for many animals: 'For most species, a brief mating season and a simple instinctive pattern make of it a seasonal disturbance with a definite routine, comparable to Christmas shopping.'[6] For human beings, sexual attraction has become something much more than a biological arrangement for propagating the species.

The 'honourable estate'[7] of marriage is the basis of immeasurable human happiness. The capacity for fidelity which not only carries on humankind to new generations, but also makes this particular kind of happiness possible, is indeed a characteristically human excellence. 'Characteristically' is still the *mot juste*. There is no question of claiming a monopoly in fidelity. Human lifelong faithfulness is best put in context by saying that human beings are pairbonding animals.[8]

For people as for animals, the possibility of pairbonding depends entirely upon our capacity to recognize one another individually and build social relationships on that. If anyone is an identifiable person, husbands and wives certainly are. Their union has evolved for the continuance of the human race. As an excellent by-product, the value of the pairbond for the well-being of individuals stands up in its own right even if there are no offspring.

The law of the land recognizes monogamy by defining marriage as 'the voluntary union for life of a man and a woman'. The church has elaborated on this by including the 'mutual help, society and comfort, that the one ought to have of the other'. Faithfulness is not a rare virtue, still less an especially Christian virtue, but is reasonably called a norm: a way of living which is natural for the kind of animal which human beings are. Evolution has brought us this way, as well as many other creatures including wolves and geese.[9] Apes, our nearest relatives, have not developed in this direction; and dogs, our closest companions, have lost the pairbonding of their wolf ancestors, having evolved to give their loyalty to people.[10]

---

[6]   Midgley, 1979
[7]   The Solemnisation of Matrimony in the *Book of Common Prayer*
[8]   Oppenheimer, *The Marriage Bond*, 1976
[9]   Lorenz, *On Aggression*, 1966, ch. XI, 'The bond'
[10] Brooks, 1987–8, pp. 35–6

Kinship to animals does not reduce human beings to 'brute beasts that have no understanding'. On the contrary, this kind of love which starts with physical attraction is the foundation for building the huge edifice of all that human romantic devotion has meant in human history. To love one person in particular, 'forsaking all other', is a good example of a vocation. Its possible deterioration into an example of idolatry or even into a tragedy does not count against its value. On the contrary, here is an illustration of the fact that excellence is more, not less, corruptible than mediocrity. The continuing urgent need for human beings to find ways of dealing with the casualties is only too real and the negative may unhappily claim more time and attention than the positive. At its best, romantic love confers magical beauty in the immediate present and is transmuted over time into the lasting blessing of secure belonging.

The book of Genesis would even suggest that the human pairbond is the primary human love. Before sin appears in the story, the man and the woman are made for each other. Holy matrimony, declares the *Book of Common Prayer,* was 'instituted by God in the time of man's innocency'. The divinely appointed union of husband and wife is first of all good for its own sake, not solely in order that they shall be fruitful and multiply. Husband and wife are to be 'one flesh'.

The Christian Gospels have a different but not incompatible primary emphasis, comparing God's love to the love of a parent rather than to the love of a spouse. In the teaching of Jesus the basic and pervasive analogy for the faithfulness of God is the way a human father loves his children. So Christians are to trust God as children trust their parents, and love one another as brothers and sisters in one family.

The doctrine that humankind was created for the love of God can be built on either of these foundations, the creation of men and women in God's image under the old covenant and their adoption as God's children under the new. The belief that evolution is the way God's creative purpose works can be comfortable with either emphasis. There is no need to decide between them nor to rank them in order of merit. The older account emphasizes that human beings really are God's creatures: the Gospels emphasize that they really are precious in God's sight. Either way, the affirmation holds good, that we matter to our Creator and to one another. What makes us godlike is our responsiveness, our minding. The foundation on which all this rests is the capacity of human beings to identify themselves and other people, and likewise to be identified as distinct individuals.

Chapter 8

Making Friends

You should not want there to be unfortunates, so that we may exercise works of mercy... He fell into need and you supplied him: you feel yourself as the giver to be the bigger man than the receiver of the gift. You should want him to be your equal, that both may be subject to the one on whom no favour can be bestowed.

St Augustine, *Homilies on I John,* VIII

Pairbonding and parenthood are excellent human possibilities, which are evidently built upon our animal heritage. In human beings they have developed conspicuously beyond their animal origins. In the process of exploring what is special about humanity, the next step moves further away from comparing people with the other animals and has more to do with contrasting them. The kind of attachment which is most distinctively human is the bond of friendship. The beasts are not entirely left behind, as anecdotes told by many pet owners testify; but here an excellence has appeared which is particularly characteristic of human beings. Friendship is as objectively real as mating and procreation, though less simply discernible.

People know what friendship means by experiencing it. If a definition is wanted, 'mutual affection and regard' has been offered.[1] Being friends is a matter of minding about one another individually and reciprocally. It includes not only wishing one another well and promoting each other's good, but also enjoying one another's company, depending happily upon one another and finding one another life-enhancing.

C.S. Lewis neatly pointed out a difference between friendship and erotic love: lovers gaze into each other's eyes, whereas friends stand side by side to look at the world.[2] There is no need to make the distinction sharp; but if it going to be blurred some care is needed. There

---

[1]   *Oxford Encyclopedic English Dictionary,* 1991
[2]   Lewis, *The Four Loves,* 1960, p. 79

are feminist ways of talking about 'tenderness' which seem to make friends into lovers rather than making lovers into friends.

The point which is worth making is that all the various kinds of human love are at their best when they have friendship as an ingredient. This is surely true of erotic relationships. Undying love is more secure and satisfying when it includes a large element of companionship as well as physical attraction. Likewise many parents find that the best part of having brought up children is finding that one has made friends with them, that they are among the people with whom one is most happy to spend time.

Even people's relationship with God can, by grace, be talked about in the language of friendship. Friendship with God is an idea most naturally applied to the mystics, but it does not have to be their special privilege. The idea of being allowed to matter to God, endowed with the blessing of God's individual loving attention, has meant much to many Christians who would not aspire to any special sanctity. Others would be fearful of any such claim. They would not dare to affirm that God speaks to them in the way God spoke to Moses 'face to face, as a man speaks to his friend'. Though in the Fourth Gospel the Lord says to his disciples, 'I have called you friends', Christians are generally happier to be content with the role the whole New Testament offers them, of being God's children. Provided that God's children are not supposed to be permanent infants but are meant to grow to maturity, the two pictures need not be incompatible nor even remote.

To give such importance to friendship in people's moral lives makes sense in the light of what Christians believe about human nature. Suppose that the Creator made the universe in such a way as to give rise to men and women. What has developed is this kind of creature who has the distinctive capacity of being able to make friends. Friendship is not peripheral. There is much more to it than a pleasant recreation for people's leisure hours. A theological understanding of friendship can be built on two basic Christian convictions, that 'God is love' and that people are made in the image and likeness of this God. It follows from these two beliefs that an integral part of being human is the capacity to enter into relationships which matter.

People can have something to say about what these relationships are like in their own experience, without claiming thereby any authority to make a contribution to biblical or to historical scholarship. On the one hand, minding about one another is not being offered here as an explanation of what the writers of the Book of Genesis really meant in their own day by the 'image of God'. On the other hand, nor are friendly relationships supposed to answer questions anthropologists may ask about how human beings first evolved. Rather, the questions about the meaning and importance of friendship in human life are *ethical* enquiries concerning what human beings mind about and what matters to them. The answers could illuminate what it means to be God's creatures.

Now some believers may begin to hear a noisy danger signal ringing. Sometimes Christians have even been instructed to give a low value to particular individual friendships. They fear that fondness for the little circle of people who matter to me can be no better than a self-centred indulgence, not at all what Christian love means. A generation who learnt Christian ethics from Anders Nygren's magisterial book *Agape and Eros* imbibed a serious distrust of special affections. The notion has spread widely that the only love which really counts is 'unmotivated', with nothing to gain, not satisfying nor rewarding. This half-truth needs critical attention because it is apt to be taken for granted by people who are not going to study the positive riches of Nygren's book.

It feels safer and more Christian not to put much emphasis on the Lord's saying to his disciples, 'I have called you friends', but rather to quote his teaching in St Luke's Gospel:

> When you give a dinner or a banquet, do not invite your friends or your brothers or your kinsmen or rich neighbours, lest they also invite you in return, and you be repaid. But when you give a feast, invite the poor, the maimed, the lame, the blind, and you will be blessed, because they cannot repay you. You will be paid at the resurrection of the just.[3]

Is this the heart of Christian teaching? The idea that one might be seriously meant to apply it in practice is not at all comfortable. It needs to be set alongside the still more difficult teaching in the same chapter of St Luke, about 'hating' the people we think we ought to love. We may well acknowledge these as hard sayings and then remind ourselves, truly, that the Lord characteristically taught by paradoxical hyperbole. We may gladly seize on to the idea that 'hate' in the Bible mans 'love less'.

If this way of responding sounds like special pleading, it can be explained more fully. There are people we naturally love without needing to be told that we should. No feeling of doing our duty, still less of looking for a reward, comes into it. We enjoy their company and we invite them into our houses, as Mary and Martha welcomed Jesus. The way we share everyday life with our friends gives us a firm basis on which we can stand and meet the world. The Lord's teaching does not cast doubt on all this.

The feast envisaged in St Luke's Gospel is a formal occasion. To give 'a dinner or a banquet' is the kind of mutual entertainment which has the proper and agreeable function of consolidating and building up people's social and public lives. The event may be delightful for some and a tedious duty for others. The guest list may, or may not, be founded on affection. There are mixed possibilities of calculated opportunism and of warm-hearted hospitality. The Lord's warning may be applied to the limitations well-behaved people impose upon their own humanity in the name of social reciprocity.[4]

What is required of Christians is not to think poorly of their ready-made natural attachments, but to transcend them. When the hard sayings about loving without looking for a reward are taken seriously they really are hard; but it would be a misunderstanding to rush into denying or deploring our everyday affections. When urgent circumstances challenge us to set our natural priorities aside, this is a real sacrifice of something valuable. The ordinary capacity to love our families and to make friends is not a concession to human weakness but belongs to God's 'very good' creation. The teachings first take it for granted that this is part of human nature, and then go on to show bolder possibilities of building on this foundation.

Rather than thinking of friendship as a second-best kind of love, we may think of it as an elementary example worked out to show the pupil how to do more difficult sums. The lesson to be learnt is the enlargement of generosity. People are meant to spread out from their given attachments to include more of God's creation in their terms of reference. Granted the cramped nature of human beings, they need this teaching and may find it difficult.

It is time for an emphatic both/and. Nygren's inspiring exposition of generous agape which seeks no reward nor even fulfilment is indeed to be gratefully taken to heart but does not have to be the whole story of what Christian love means. *Agape*, the love that gives, may be praised without disparaging the other loves which have been called *eros* and *philia*, the love that wants and the love that

---

[4]   Oppenheimer, 1983, pp. 132–3

appreciates.[5] It is something of a limitation in the English language that all these meanings are generally lumped together by the one word 'love'. When the attempt is made to disentangle them, *eros* and *philia* are too easily dealt with by being treated as irreconcilable rivals to *agape*. Christian loyalty says, 'Choose agape' and seems to say, 'Give up the others.' The positive 'up with this' appears to imply a negative 'down with that'.

Nygren is far from saying 'down with eros'. On the contrary, his measured account of St Augustine's synthesis of agape and eros into the idea of *caritas* [6] is one of the strengths of his book; but still in the end it is only agape which he allows to count as Christian love. The difference of emphasis is subtle but goes deep. For Nygren, eros turns out to be a sort of splendid failure. Meantime *philia*, the love of friends, is hardly mentioned, and surely one may dare to count this as a failing.

It does not help in sorting out the different kinds of love that in ordinary language 'erotic' means, not so much selfish, as essentially physical and unspiritual. All the glories and potential embarrassments of sexual ethics are brought into discussions of many every-day affectionate relationships to which they may be entirely irrelevant. So Nygren's argument about eros in his sense, the kind of love that looks for a return, is short-circuited. When discussions about the significance of body and spirit have taken over, it feels naive to insist that the excellence of friendship is being overlooked.

Can individual attachments have anything to do with Christian love? The Lord's human life evidently did not include eros in the sense of erotic relationships. Whatever romantic interests film-makers may see fit to attribute to him, in the Gospels he is celibate. It by no means appears however that he avoided particular friendships. Among his disciples Peter, James and John emerge as his especial companions. In the Fourth Gospel, he wept for Lazarus; and one of his followers could be picked out as 'beloved'.

To Nygren, this strand in Christian teaching which is willing to honour specific human loves is the beginning of a false emphasis in Christian ethics, set right at last by Luther.[7] Nygren presents a balanced case. He acknowledges and emphasizes that the Johannine version of agape as love for the brethren has 'a depth, warmth and

---

[5]   See Lewis, *The Four Loves*, 1960. The fourth love is *storge*, human affection, of which family love is the main example.

[6]   Nygren, 1969, Part II, ch. II, e.g. p. 451–2

[7]   Nygren, 1969, Part II, ch. VI

intimacy that are without parallel elsewhere ... Agape is the *fellowship* of love.' But he can give this approach only limited approval, for he insists that if Christian love is shrunk to brotherly love it loses 'its original unmotivated character'. He sees affectionate warmth as gained at the cost of a restrictive narrowness, including brethren but not outsiders, still less enemies. What Nygren cannot find here is St Paul's grateful astonishment that he, the 'lost and estranged' persecutor, should be the object of God's unconditional love.[8]

The warning may be accepted but a converse warning is needed just as much. Nygren's gratitude for God's miraculous paradoxical love for sinners is also gained at a cost. 'Unmotivated' is not personal enough to do justice to the generosity of agape (see above p. 47). Its negative form gives it away. God's love is defined by what it is not. To insist that God loves without expecting any response suggests that God never really minds. Must God's creatures be glad to be loved with such detachment? God's agape is presented as so lofty that we must not suppose that God wants anything as wholeheartedly as we do. Is it really more Christian to be entirely disinterested, or would it be too near to being *un*interested?[9] Traherne's surprise that 'It is very strange that God should want' (see above p. 47 and below p. 132), is more satisfying and more biblical than Nygren's certainty that God has nothing to gain, that the Creator expects no satisfaction from creation.

Wanting is one way in which God's creatures are like their Maker. If this is paradoxical, so be it. It may even help, not to smooth over the paradox but to sharpen it by thinking of God's love as including *partiality*.[10] 'Partial' is not the exact opposite of 'impartial'. 'I am rather partial to garlic' does not mean that I am unfair to horseradish. It means that here is something I choose for its own sake because I like it. It should be illuminating, not outrageous, to believe that God's love, and some good human loves, include this sort of partiality: choosing people for their own sakes.

Christian understanding could be improved if we took a rest from always using the all-purpose blanket word 'love'. 'Liking' could do with being rehabilitated as a basic, not trivial, category which is central to what friendship means. Might we dare to apply this to God's love and say that as well as loving us with an unmotivated love, God can like us for our own sakes? If we could grasp the idea that God is,

---

[8]   Nygren, 1969, pp. 154–5
[9]   See Oppenheimer, 1983, ch. 11
[10]   Oppenheimer, 1983, ch. 14

so to say, on our side, this would offer a corrective to the one-sided notion that our sinfulness is all there is of us. God loves individual people and will not hold their misdeeds against them, quite differently from the impersonal mercy Heine on his deathbed is said to have taken for granted, 'Dieu me pardonnera: c'est son métier'.[11] When St Paul said that 'God is for us',[12] this could mean, not only judging us mercifully, but seeing how things look from our point of view, as a friend would.

The suggestion that God's love includes partiality may be less shocking in the light of God's infinity. Unlike finite human beings, God can be impartial to all and partial to every single one. A primary school child who said regretfully 'I haven't got time to like all my friends' was up against the narrow limitations of earthly life, which are not all caused by sin. If human love in heaven is more like God's love, this need not mean becoming less individual, but having more scope to fulfil the manifold particular loves of which human beings are capable.

If it is in order to appreciate Nygren thus far and no farther, loyal Christians may happily make room in Christian ethics for *philia* as well as for agape and eros. They may celebrate friendship wholeheartedly as a characteristic human excellence and may hope to understand all the better what it means to be made in God's image.

There emerges now a contrary danger of setting friendship on a pedestal. A high view of friendship runs the risk of distinguishing it too boldly from the kinds of love which we share with the other animals. Because pairbonding and parenthood are manifested in plain physical ways, it is a short step to the notion that friendship is a more 'spiritual' kind of love than these. Are people not only more sophisticated than the beasts, but holier? That would be a dangerously false kind of spirituality. If the danger is grasped in the way one is supposed to grasp nettles, it may turn out positively to shed light on the meaning of the image of God.

'Spiritual' is a slippery word. 'Spirit' may be used in simple contrast with 'body', to mean some kind of being whose existence for good or ill is not part of the physical world. If materialism were true there would in reality be no spirits. But 'spiritual' often offers information, not just about fact but about value. It can mean something like 'sacred'. To call friendship 'spiritual' would be to believe, like Keats, in 'the holiness of the heart's affections'.[13] Whether one

---

[11] *Oxford Dictionary of Quotations*, 1999
[12] *Romans* 8.31
[13] Letter to Benjamin Bailey, 22 November 1817

warms to his romanticism or finds it ethically risky to set human love so high, he need not be taken to mean that holy love must belong to a world separated from the material world. The heart's affections may be both spiritual and physical, and human friendship, however blessed, need not be something apart from our animal nature.

Human beings are indeed physical creatures and all our relationships, lofty or lowly, have a physical basis. It is more than a metaphor to say that we 'keep in touch' with our friends. We live in one material world and communicate by bodily means far more diverse than loving embraces.

More basic to the life of bodily creatures even than mating and procreating is taking nourishment. Just as the pairbond and parenthood have evolved beyond their animal origins, so the ways in which human beings feed one another have emerged from, and developed beyond, the ways in which animals bring food for their young or their mates or their hunting packs. People do more than provide one another with nourishment: they prepare meals and eat them with more or less formality. John Habgood, discussing how 'Human beings are inveterate improvers' pointed out as 'an obvious example' the taming of fire; and drew attention to the fact that 'Cooking clearly distinguishes human beings from other animals'.[14] Obvious as this may be, it has been easily overlooked by a good many male thinkers, who have been more used to emphasize such traditional human abilities as reasoning and tool-using than to take into account the everyday organization of meals.

In human society, whether primitive or sophisticated, a conspicuous and natural manifestation of friendship is the practice of hospitality. To be hosts and guests is as characteristic a human role as to be parents and children or husbands and wives, less fundamental of course but especially distinctive of humanity. Karl Barth pointed out that in the natural world 'the big fish does not greet the little fish but eats it'.[15]

Like friendship itself, expressing friendship by hospitality has value in human life which is much more than trivial. It is plain enough to see how purposeful friendly sociability is useful to us as a species: but, more than that, eating meals together can have a deeper significance which may justly be called sacramental.[16]

---

[14] Habgood, *The Concept of Nature*, 2002, p. 113
[15] Barth, *Ethics*, 1981, p. 142
[16] Oppenheimer, 1994, pp. 150–1

The practice of hospitality is an example of a characteristic human activity which means more than meets the eye, which signifies more than the evident bare facts. A welcoming table can be, literally, a human sacrament, according to the definition of a sacrament given in the *Book of Common Prayer* , 'an outward and visible sign of an inward and spiritual grace' (the Catechism).

Because Christians are so used to lining up before an altar to kneel and receive a consecrated wafer and sip of wine, they may lose touch with the basis of their Holy Communion in a real meal, the supper the Lord arranged for his friends before he was brutally removed from them. The meaning of the last supper is illuminated by being set in the context of the many occasions when Jesus took bread, gave thanks to God, broke it and shared it.[17] At all those meals, eating and drinking together became a blessing: in other words, a means of grace.

In the Thanksgiving from which has developed the Christian Eucharist, Jesus consecrated the bread and wine on the table, which already signified his hospitality, to signify his body and his blood, the life he was about to give. Austin Farrer explained, 'He gave them the sacrament by eating with them; he made it their salvation by his death'.[18] The authority required for this to be believable is the Christian experience of his rising from the dead.

Whatever is to be believed about the empty tomb, the Gospel accounts of the Resurrection emphasize that the meal we call the Last Supper was not after all the last supper. The stories insist that the life which the Lord lived with the people who were his friends was continued by his returning in bodily reality.[19] In the Gospel according to St Luke, he asks them for something to eat and they produce for him a piece of broiled fish. He made himself known to two disconsolate disciples when he broke bread at Emmaus. The Fourth Gospel describes his hospitality in a picnic by the lakeside. These stories ought not to be written off as naïve by people who prefer a more spiritual faith. They express the conviction that for human beings spiritual reality is grounded in physical reality.

To believe that the Eucharist is a dependable renewal of the meals which the Lord and his companions shared provides a meaning for the ancient idea of 'real presence' which leaves aside the controversial ramifications developed by divided Christians.[20]

---

[17]   Including the feeding of the 5,000
[18]   Farrer, 'The Eucharist in I Corinthians', 1968, p. 31
[19]   Oppenheimer, 1994, p. 156–7
[20]   Oppenheimer, 1994, p. 148–9

His was the word that spake it,
He took the bread and brake it,
And what his word did make it,
I do believe and take it.[21]

Everything that has developed, in all the succeeding centuries, from the supper in the upper room depends upon the distinctive human capacity to make material things into sacraments by endowing them with transcendent meaning.

---

[21] Verse ascribed to Queen Elizabeth I

Chapter 9

Hoping

He asked life of thee, and thou gavest him a long life:
even for ever and ever ...

Psalm 21.4

The Christian sacrament of Holy Communion seems to have left the animal creation a long way behind. Whatever skills animals have, they surely do not take part in holy rites. Has discontinuity now prevailed over continuity? It would be dishonest to deny the possibility that it really might. Humankind is said to be 'made in God's image' and to pay no heed to that early theological affirmation would be both unrealistic and ungracious.

There is still the strenuous imperative of both/and: *both* to recognize gladly that animals are fellow-creatures and have gifts as remarkable as ours, *and* to attend to whatever turns out to be truly special about our humanity.We live human lives and rejoice in our human gifts, which of course we find especially remarkable. Such grateful loyalty may gladly acknowledge that our human excellences are different only in degree from the excellences of other animals.

Descartes' suggestion that animals are not fellow creatures but automata is indeed 'monstrous'.[1] Not only in practice but also in theory we can work on the ordinary and natural assumption that animals have conscious experiences and mind about what happens. Of course the lives of many animals *matter* to them. People who argue that a rabbit caught in a trap does not really feel anything may themselves be called 'unfeeling'.

Nor do we suppose that animal experience has to be entirely limited to physical sensations, hunger, thirst, pleasure, warmth, cold, pain. It is not sentimental to believe that animal relationships bear some analogy to ours. Anyone who has enjoyed Konrad Lorenz's descriptions of the courtship, bonding, fidelity and bereavements of

---

[1]   See above, p. 30

greylag geese may well be encouraged to be more anthropomorphic, not less, about animal lives. Lorenz himself put it with due caution: 'It is on principle impossible to make any scientifically legitimate assertions about the subjective experiences of animals' but yet 'We are convinced that animals do have emotions, though we shall never be able to say exactly what these emotions are'.[2] Surely mammals and birds in some way care about as well as care for their offspring; and pairbonding creatures have some sort of feeling, more than simply sexual, for their own mates. To go on from there to describe animals as being like us by having friends looks more riskily metaphorical than to recognize that they manifestly have parents and mates; but it is hardly metaphorical to say that they are glad of each other's company. For some animals, grooming one another is a kind of conversation. Animals who have been housed together and then parted truly miss and mourn their companions. Animals who bring each other food are 'companions' in the original sense of 'bread- sharers'.

As we move to and fro between appreciating likenesses between human beings and animals and searching out real distinctions, Mary Midgley's warning against talking easily about '"the difference between man and animal" without saying *which* animal' (see above p. 25) is even more to the purpose. In many ways we are akin to apes and, it seems, to dolphins; in other ways we have more in common with birds.

Lynne Sharpe in *Creatures Like Us?* is eloquent about the capacity of horses and dogs to form real relationships with human beings. She sets much less store on our genetic nearness to chimpanzees: who, even if they succeed in acquiring some human language, remain creatures who are not enough 'like us' to share our domestic lives. On the other hand, Frans de Waal in *Good Natured* offers telling and intriguing illustrations of the social behaviour of the great apes themselves, which seems to lay the foundations for what we mean by morality. He offers examples of sympathy, reciprocity and the handling of aggression. There is plenty of scope for comparing and contrasting, preferring both/and to either/or, and declining to over-simplify the variety of the creation. The comparisons do not refute the contrasts but shed light upon them.

There comes a time for putting the emphasis on contrast. The analogy between human and animal relationships does seem to break down when we recognize the long-term ethical dimension of human affection, which seems not to apply to animal caring. A mother animal may die for her young; but once they have lived to be adults

[2]   Lorenz, 1966, ch. XI

these particular individuals generally cease to play a special role in her life. Animals have mates; but they do not have spouses. The 'mutual help, society and comfort' provided by animal attachment is not expected to include the whole range of what the marriage bond means for human wives and husbands. The intricate amicable relationships of social animals fall a good way short of the kind of significant organized hospitality which is a characteristic aspect of human living.[3] Chimpanzees do not really give tea parties. A wolf sharing his kill with the pack is answering the question, 'What's for dinner?' not asking the question, 'May I have the pleasure of your company?'

It would be false humility to disregard the human capacity to reach a new stage and to transcend the gifts which belong to our animal heritage. The stage further is the ability of human beings to find significance in life, to consider the meaning of life and even to bestow meaning on life. We are not only valuable, we understand what it is to be valuable, in a way that other animals surely do not.

Along with the knowledge that we are valuable comes the knowledge that we are mortal. When we see other creatures die, we are aware that this is going to be our own fate. Since human beings too are physical creatures, it is plain that they are not naturally imperishable. Human parents are obliged to admit to their children that people are not going to live for ever and somehow help them to come to terms with the idea of death.

Knowing that we are valuable, we rebel against our mortality. People normally want to go on living for a long time and to see their cherished hopes being fulfilled. They do not readily abandon the ancient hope of living for ever and ever. At least as far back as homo sapiens Neanderthalis, human beings have buried dead bodies with reverence.[4] From the idea that a corpse is not to be treated as if it were merely a thing, it is not a long step to some concept of 'spirit'.

Though it is evident that all living bodies decay and die, it is no wonder that people who value their lives persist in asking whether death has to be final. Throughout most of human history people have decided that it does not. The belief that we may survive death is a resilient world view which mature human beings have responsibly held, which is anyway not to be put aside as merely a story for children. Thinking people today who hope to reaffirm life after

[3]   See de Waal, *Good Natured*, 1996. But see also Charlotte Uhlenbroek, *Talking with Animals*, 2002, p. 229: 'Offering food to an other individual is such a universally understood gesture of friendship that it easily transcends the species barrier.'

[4]   See *Encyclopedia of Human Evolution and Prehistory*, 1988, p. 370.

death convincingly, rather than take it on trust, have to embark first on quite a long journey.

That journey may not go by the obvious dualist route, looking for detachable souls able to survive the death of their bodies.[5] The notion of the soul as a *pattern* is more promising. But because religious people have been so sure that their hope for a future life depends upon their twofoldness, the concept of the immortal soul needs more attention before it can be set aside. Many Christians have been glad to slot dualism into their thinking. They have found it easy to adopt Descartes' view, that over and above our physical flesh and blood there is some part of us which is not physical but spiritual. They nominate this immortal soul, which we have and animals presumably lack, as the important part of a human being.

Believers have outgrown the idea that God literally sculpted Adam out of clay and then physically 'breathed into his nostrils the breath of life'. They have not outgrown the conviction that the meaning of the myth is true. They take it to signify that human creatures are spiritual, because God endows them with souls as well as bodies. In some frames of mind, dualism has looked like commonsense. Religious faith can seem to depend upon a compulsory certainty that what survives death must be the soul. Christian believers add, more or less emphatically, that the body will rise again in the end and soul and body will be re-united.

The straightforward prospect of dead people waking up again after death, roused by the Last Trump as their alarm clock, getting up out of the grave after a refreshing sleep and despatched to heaven or hell or maybe purgatory, is a primitive fancy. The more sophisticated dualist account is that when it has become clear that our mortal bodies are not going to get up any more, our immortal souls will be ready to take over. A little philosophical thought can render that version just as unconvincing. It seems easy enough to imagine a spirit inhabiting a body, but once they are taken apart it is not so easy to put a live human being together again. Descartes surely made a category mistake when he suggested that the role of the pineal gland might be to link soul and body, as if they were two *things* which could be separated or joined. What was the point of our Creator making us in this double way? If we have souls, why do we need bodies too?

---

[5]   I first developed this argument in 'Life after death', and explored it more fully in *Looking Before and After,* especially ch. 3.

Dualism is not as obvious as traditionalists have tended to think.
G.R. Dunstan called it 'that tiresome language' which 'has infected
Western piety and thought'.[6] The value of human beings cannot be
understood by taking them to pieces. Believers ought to listen to
those philosophers who ask persistently how these immaterial
things called 'souls' can find one another or recognize one another
without their physical bodies. Peter Strawson argued in 1959 that a
disembodied person no longer has any purchase on the world and
will have to 'live much in the memories of the personal life he did
lead'. 'No doubt', he commented, ironically but perceptively, 'it is
for this reason that the orthodox have wisely insisted upon the resurrection of the body.'[7]

It is bodies, things in space and time, that we can see, hear, touch.[8]
We can pick them out and tell them apart. A body is a sort of home
base which places a person in the real world. A disembodied immaterial spirit would have, literally, no foot-hold in earthly reality, no
hands for keeping in touch, no eyes for seeing anything in particular,
no ears for hearing what anyone else says: in other words, no point of
view. If our souls cannot manage any better than this, they are not
much use.

It is worth trying to do justice to the sense of liberation it gives to
stop thinking of people in this way, as souls plus-or-minus bodies. In
the mid-twentieth century Professor Ryle's *Concept of Mind* (1949)
instigated a powerful revolt against dualism. Christians would do
well to adopt his mistrust of the 'ghost in the machine', rather than
fighting defensive actions to try to rescue our immortal souls.

If they put dualism aside, what they could say would be both more
convincing and more exhilarating. A human being, a child of God, is
one person. We are whole people, living in one material world, keeping in touch with one another as fellow creatures, not indirectly but
directly.[9] God has created a universe with an almost infinite diversity of embodied living beings. People are no more, and no less, than
the most complex and subtle of these.

This way of affirming the complete person is not traditional
sceptical materialism. We can still talk about the soul as much as we
like, thinking of it as the whole person considered spiritually. We

[6] Dunstan, 1981, p. 6
[7] Strawson, *Individuals*, 1959, pp. 115–6
[8] I discussed this problem about disembodied spirits in *Incarnation and Immanence*, 1973, pp. 26–9 and in *Looking Before and After*, ch. 5, pp. 57–9 and p. 67.
[9] See Oppenheimer, 1979, p. 132

can ask when embodied beings began to *be* spiritual beings, in history or in individual life, rather than when they began to *have* souls as detachable items.

That still does not explain whether it eventually means anything to think of me as a spirit, once I have stopped believing that my body has a soul which belongs to it? If I live as a whole, must it follow that I die as a whole? People who have come to look on the notion of the immortal soul as wishful thinking have had to find ways of enduring a more sceptical climate, whether with the wistfulness of Matthew Arnold on Dover Beach, or the bravado of Bertrand Russell, who believed that when he died he would rot, but who scorned to succumb to panic.[10] Sceptical humanism shows itself at its best in the honest courage of a secular funeral, which instead of trite comfort is able to make the affirmation that life goes on and that one generation can make way gracefully for another. The idea of 'spirituality' has not disappeared but has even come into its own, offering a terminology in which people with or without religious faith may recognize that reductive materialism is not the only alternative to orthodoxy. People who aspire to a more robust religious faith, or whose cast of mind is more prosaic, should 'tread softly' rather than trample on other people's dreams.[11]

All this makes opinions about the nature and value of human beings less polarized but more confused. There is an honourable strand in Christian thinking which finds the idea of another life more expendable than it has traditionally been.[12] Radical thinkers, who find time-honoured Christian beliefs about heaven simply too naïve, do not necessarily abandon their faith in God but continue to affirm it, with evident integrity. They take an austere moral stance, that what human beings are for is to love God, and that attempts to imagine heaven are a distraction from the one thing needful. They have the ancient Israelites on their side, who worshipped God in this life without any clear conviction of another life to come. Something has gone wrong if God is utilized as a telephone or a ferryboat, useful for getting in touch with the beloved people who have gone.

Christians who still believe that there is more to their Christian hope than their present ambiguous life which is due to be extinguished find that the arguments they offer are treated as debating

---

[10]   Russell, 'A free man's worship', 1917, pp. 46–7
[11]   W.B. Yeats 'Aedh wishes for the cloths of heaven'
[12]   It was Dr Leslie Houlden who made me take this point of view with respectful seriousness.

points and that their appeals to the teaching of Christ are suspect as 'proof-texting'. To hanker after heaven and specify the character of a better world than this is supposed to be both intellectually and morally dubious.

We are back in Alice's garden, where once again the only way of arriving at the proposed destination is to set off paradoxically in the opposite direction. Alice's garden is a good place to be for a Christian theologian. Rather than persisting with hopeful short cuts which turn out not to lead to the promised land, it would be better to try some lateral thinking. To take a roundabout way to reach one's destination is not unfaithful.

It is a basic Christian principle that people have to let go, and let go completely, of what they hope to keep, before their possession of it can be fulfilled. On the one hand, people who crave for a happy afterlife need to give their attention to worshipping God and stop specifying what sort of heaven they require. On the other hand, people who long for spiritual experience should attend first to other people, rather than follow the frustrating route of resolute devoutness.

Heaven must be something different from the prospect of simply going on as we are. The answer St Paul gave to the question 'How are the dead raised?' was, 'You foolish man, what you sow does not come to life, *unless it dies.*'[13] That is a text on which Christian encouragement really can be founded. Wherever a future heaven may be, it is on the other side of death.[14] Before we can find our souls or anyone else's soul, we have to be lost and lose each other. The heart of Christian hope is that what people grab they lose, but that what they give up is to be splendidly given back to them.

The hunt for the immortal soul leads into a dead end. Once the argument is stuck here, neither superstitious spiritualism, relying on ghosts, nor defeatist scepticism, settling for machines, is a good way on. Now it is time to pick up again the hopeful suggestion that our souls are not *objects* at all, whether durable or perishable.[15] The soul is no *thing*, but nor is it *nothing*. It really is well described as a *pattern*, the renewable pattern of the whole person.

A human being is a whole and when death comes the whole person does die, like a computer program switched off. Faith would do well not to depend upon the kind of surviving spirit which stays and

---

[13] *I Corinthians* 15.36
[14] See Oppenheimer, 1979, p. 334
[15] See Oppenheimer, 1979, p. 333

haunts the scene or boards Charon's boat to the underworld. The computer image offers a more promising way of picturing how death need not be the end. People have the kind of fragility and the kind of durability which software has. The Creator, who values each person, has saved the data and will re-establish the pattern, maybe after a lapse of time, in different hardware. It is fitting to be hopefully agnostic about what heaven may be like. There is nothing wrong with enlivening one's imagination with a variety of pictures, all the better when they are evidently naïve and creatively fanciful rather than deceptively literal.

The key affirmation is: God-given resurrection rather than natural immortality. The question is not, What sort of substance is a soul? but What sort of God is our Maker? Our tradition offers an answer: the God of Abraham, Isaac and Jacob, who is not the God of the dead but of the living.

Chapter 10

Speaking – Human Glory

'The question is', said Alice, 'whether you *can* make words mean
so many different things.'

Lewis Carroll, *Through the Looking-Glass*, ch. VI

Dualism separates human beings from 'the beasts that perish',
endowing us with immortal souls which qualify us for eternal life in
God's presence. If we stop insisting on this doubleness of body and
soul, we should be glad to unite our split selves and live as whole
persons in the physical world. The corollary to be willingly accepted
is to weaken the time-honoured contrast between Man and the other
creatures.

Someone who has given up dualism may be inclined to give up the
whole idea of human souls. It appears that we are 'only animals'. A
better alternative is to give up the 'only' and think less dismissively
about our fellow creatures. Human beings are living bodies in much
the same way as animals are living bodies. Once we take to heart the
idea that the soul is not a separate thing added on to the body but a
pattern,[1] we can also take to heart the idea that to be, so to say,
'ensouled' is a matter of degree. Might the pattern, not only of
human lives, but of some animal lives turn out to be renewable? At
least the kinds of animals who are endowed with responsiveness
cannot be confidently denied some place of their own in the kingdom of heaven.

Strong clear self-consciousness would not be a needful qualification. A creature could be a 'pattern of lovability' without knowing it,
recognizable to others though not to itself. If the essential criterion
for counting as 'spiritual' is *being* a soul, not *having* a soul, then the
quality to look for is some minimal capacity to respond to what is

---

[1]   Oppenheimer, 1988, ch. 7; and above p. 38

going on. It hardly makes sense to say that a creature who is never going to be able to mind about what happens could be a child of God.

The primary ingredient of responsiveness is the ability to make identifications. All the social relationships natural to people and to many animals, companionship, pairbonding, caring for offspring, depend upon the decisive ability we certainly share with many other creatures, the ability to recognize one another. Recognition may mean no more than 'Here is this again'. Before there could be any relationships which we could think of as loving, let alone as giving meaning to life, something beyond elementary identification is needed: the crucial capacity for two-way communication.

Animals, of course, communicate with one another, in ways more sophisticated that people often recognize;[2] but it cannot be said that animals 'possess a language in the true sense of the word'.[3] Only in fables and fairy stories are they expected to talk. The structures of their throats are not adapted for the fine control required for the subtle complexities of human words. Capacity for language has still more to do with the structures of human brains, in which it seems that two small areas govern the power to speak. By developing 'the anatomical basis for spoken complex language'[4] human beings really have evolved beyond other creatures. The article on Hominidae in the fifteenth edition of the *Encyclopedia Britannica* postulates 'that language arises in a species in which auditory control over vocalization is sufficiently developed to permit individuals to imitate each other's sounds.' 'Symbolic meaning, however crude, would not be attached to particular sounds if one animal could not imitate vocalizations in others.'

The ability to produce complicated recognizable sounds is not the whole story about what differentiates human beings from 'dumb animals'. Parrots talk distinctly, without understanding; whereas an individual who has suffered trauma to the brain may be unable to utter words, without loss of understanding. Aphasia may leave comprehension intact. So the question has been raised whether apes, who are much more like human beings than parrots are, have failed to develop the use of language only because they lack the physiological apparatus for speaking? People have wondered whether to think of them, so to say, as aphasic. There was excitement about

---

[2]   See e.g. Uhlenbroek, 2002
[3]   Lorenz, *King Solomon's Ring*, 1952, ch. 8
[4]   Diamond, 1991, pp.46–8

Washoe, the ape who was taught to make some use of American Sign Language;[5] but what had she really learned? Even apart from the doubts about the narrow limits of the vocabulary and grammar she could manage, her linguistic attainments were wholly dependent upon human input. She had no mother tongue to pass on to succeeding generations.[6]

Konrad Lorenz illuminated the intricate ways in which animal communication is both like and unlike human language, more convincingly than by taking sides.[7] He sorted out some of the subtleties of what it may mean to say that animals understand words and even use them; and conveyed the wonder of animal behaviour all the better because he was not making a case but relishing the real world in its complexity.

Whatever qualifications need to be introduced, the full use of language is a basic distinction, on which depends most other significant advantages which human beings may claim over other animals. The best way to bring out the difference language makes is to look at language in action. For instance, to pick up the way I have just used the word 'significant' and ring the changes on it may shed light on what is, indeed, so significant about language.

The meanings of 'significance' range from everyday to profound. A 'significant advantage', at its simplest, is an appreciable advantage. Likewise a 'meaningful' advantage may mean no more than an advantage which is not merely trivial. Beyond this prosaic use, either 'signifying' or 'meaning' may evidently have a more high-powered import. Human beings have the capacity to recognize more profound significance, deeper meaning. 'I realise how much music *means* to her'. This grander use of 'meaningful' says something about the capacities of people: but curiously enough it is not this loftier kind of meaning which sheds light on the significance for humankind of being language-users. To announce solemnly that people find meaning in their lives may not amount to more than a high-falutin' way of saying that they are happy.

The most significant kind of significance is more ordinary than the deeply meaningful. It is the everyday possibility of one occurrence meaning something else. 'When I smell onions cooking, that's a sign that dinner is nearly ready'. 'When the engine makes rattling noises, that means trouble'. It is this prosaic sense of the verb 'to mean'

---

[5]   E.g. Linden, *Apes, Men and Language*, 1976, pp. 53-4
[6]   Hearne, *Adam's Task*, 1986, pp. 18–20, 32–41
[7]   Lorenz, 1952, pp. 76–89

which turns out to indicate something particularly distinctive, indeed significant, about human beings. Promising smells wafting from the kitchen may mean dinner, but so may a bell or a voice calling us to eat. Domestic animals may learn to respond to such signals, but human beings can arrange them. To notice the everyday fact that people can bestow meaning, that they can appoint one thing to signify, to stand for, to mean, something *else*, is to identify a human capacity which opens up whole realms of understanding.

Edwin Muir was not going in for thoughtless 'speciesism' when he wrote that animals have no words 'to plant a foot upon'.[8] He was recognizing a characteristic ability of humankind: that we can, as it were, use words as stepping stones for making expeditions beyond the present. Ludwig Wittgenstein at one stage said something very like this in cold prose: 'The limits of my language mean the limits of my world.'[9] Turned round into a positive statement, this can become an affirmation that the capacity to use words to carry us outside the present moment has a lot to do with what it means to live a human life. The philosopher H.H. Price used to call this capacity 'thinking in absence'. He explained what this means: when we use words as symbols, 'concepts are brought to mind by means of concepts which are not instances of them'.[10] The *Encyclopedia Britannica* describes symbol-use as giving 'arbitrary meaning to material objects'.

One way of not taking language for granted is to consider an exceptional case. Helen Keller became both deaf and blind as a toddler and her governess found a way of showing her what words are, pouring water over her hand while spelling out the word 'water' on her fingers.[11] So she suddenly understood the link between the thought of water and the sign for it. By using the word, she could summon up the idea of water, for herself or for other people, whether there was any water there or not. From this beginning she entered into the human world.

This ability to think about something when it is not there is a *significant* fact about human beings. We can think, know, believe, wonder, feel, plan about what is not immediately before us. We are not confined to the present moment, to our immediate time and place. We are not stuck in our own selves, because we can enter into the experience of other people. In a way, the whole universe becomes ours.

---

[8]   Edwin Muir, 'The animals' *Collected Poems 1921–1958*; quoted by permission of Faber & Faber.

[9]   Wittgenstein, *Tractatus Logico-Philosophicus*, 1922, 5.6

[10] Price, *Thinking and Experience*, 1953, p. 254. See Oppenheimer, 2001, p. 52

[11] Keller, *The Story of My Life*, 1902. See *Encyclopaedia Britannica*, Vol. 8, p. 1026

When we claim this human capability as characteristic, the word 'characteristic' is precise. Plenty of instances can be given of other animals who are aware of features of the world not immediately present to them. Peter Gärdenfors describes how differently snakes and cats hunt because cats have 'object permanence'.[12] A snake has to use three separate kinds of sensation, sight, smell and touch, to chase, catch and eat mice, because it has no image of an enduring mouse to help it to 'predict that a mouse that runs under one side of an armchair will come out the other side'. Meantime a cat can sit and wait expectantly outside a mouse hole. Family pets apprehend not only objects but meanings, comprehending human words and responding to them. Lynne Sharpe tells how her dogs show by their behaviour that they have understood from her actions yesterday evening that an outing is going to happen today.[13] In a book about animal communication called *Talking with Animals*, Charlotte Uhlenbroek describes the 'waggle dance' of bees as 'a truly symbolic form of communication, a signal that provides information about something separated in both space and time'.[14] Here is meaning 'in absence' indeed, though it cannot be counted as 'thinking'.

Humanity need not be unique to be marvellous. However like or unlike we are to other living creatures, our human use of language is fit to be celebrated as a wonderful endowment. We share it, at least to some extent, with apes and dogs who understand what we say, presumably not at all with slugs. Language depends upon complex recognition, 're-knowing', both of items in the world and of the words which we and other people use to bring them to mind.[15] This is what H.H. Price explained in the language of a philosopher and Edwin Muir expressed in poetry. It is 'with names' that human beings call the world into existence.

It looks as if human beings are unique in actively teaching language to our young. Human babies begin to talk by babbling, and babbling develops into speech with the help of the loving feedback given by proud mothers. Charlotte Uhlenbroek notices how important in the upbringing of human children is repeatedly telling them the names of things around them (p. 214). Adults teach children what words mean. Disabilities which impede human verbal com-

[12] Gärdenfors, *How Homo Became Sapiens*, 2003, pp. 36–7
[13] Sharpe, 2005, pp. 143–4
[14] Uhlenbroek, 2002, p. 200
[15] See Savage-Rumbaugh *et al.*, 'Language, speech, tools and writing', 2001, especially pp. 276–8, on how language makes it possible to have awareness of a shared world.

munication, from ordinary deafness to rarer autism, have a particular severity, maybe all the more damaging for not being outwardly conspicuous. The instruction of the most highly-educated scholar has not included any more remarkable lesson than speech, which each of us learned before we were old enough to remember being taught it.

Humanists may claim the marvel of words as something after their own hearts. Christian humanists need have no quarrel with their enthusiasm but will want to go on to connect the human gift of language with the meaning of the image of God. The particular glory of speech is a marvel with thoroughly Biblical foundations. In the first chapter of the Book of Genesis, God is not introduced first of all as King, Judge, or even Father, but as Speaker. 'Let there be light'. Everything begins with God's verbal command. Believers are not committed to imagining their God as having vocal chords. They do not have to ask what language God spoke or who was there to obey. The belief to which they are committed, when they affirm that God is personal, is that God is a Communicator. Human beings are communicators because they are made in God's image.

When in the fullness of time Christians came to believe that the same God who had summoned the creation into existence had entered into the creation to save it, their primary image was of course that God the Father sent his *Son*. That primary image of a beloved emissary was not the only image for God's dealings with humanity. The fourth Gospel, echoing the Book of Genesis, proclaims that 'in the beginning' was the *Word*. According to this image, it was the Word spoken by God the Creator which 'became flesh and dwelt among us': a sort of heavenly mixed metaphor come true. To call Jesus God's Word is to call him God's means of communication.

The Greek for word, 'Logos', is notoriously difficult to translate into English, since it means either 'speech' or 'reason' and offers a hard choice between them. Whatever profound significance theologians may find in 'the Logos', it conveys at least the idea that God gets in touch with human creatures. It is in keeping with this image of God as Speaker that when Peter, James and John were shown the vision of Jesus transfigured, what they saw and heard was not Jesus enthroned, but Jesus talking with Moses and Elijah.[16]

In the Epistle to the Hebrews the conjunction of creating and communicating recurs. The God who made the universe spoke 'in many

[16] *Mark* 9.2–4

and various ways' by the prophets and at last 'by a Son'.[17] God's Word is not personified here, but God's making and God's verbal communication still belong together. It is the Son by whom God speaks to humankind, 'through whom also he created the worlds. He is the reflection of God's glory and the exact imprint of God's very being, and he sustains all things by his powerful word.'

This is picture-language, metaphorical not literal: Word in the fourth Gospel, reflection, imprint, upholder, in the Epistle to the Hebrews. From the divine point of view these metaphysical descriptions of Jesus Christ may be as naive as the simple mythology of Genesis 3, where the Lord God walks in the garden in the cool of the day, hoping to enjoy the company of the human creatures.

God calls to Adam, 'Where are you?' But Adam has sinned and is hiding among the leaves, rather than being glad to see his Maker. The ancient narrative is about how communication between people and their Creator is impaired. This fact is too clear, whatever myth or history we invoke to account for it. Yet the whole Biblical saga of God's people assumes that communication is not destroyed.

There has always been the conviction that God sometimes addresses chosen individuals in words, saying things like, 'Whom shall I send, and who will go for us?'[18] People use words to talk to God. They say things like: 'O knit my heart unto thee, that I may fear thy name'[19] or: 'Speak, Lord, for thy servant heareth'[20] or even: 'My God, my God, why hast thou forsaken me?'[21] For Christians the story culminates in the strange renewal of communication, promised but unexpected, when the Word has been made flesh and God-made-man, at the brink of death, picked up the Psalmist's human words of dereliction.[22] The Cross and the rising from the dead, taken together, become the pledge[23] that the Creator is in touch with the human creatures which the universe has brought forth and will not leave them comfortless.

[17] *Hebrews* 1.1–3
[18] *Isaiah* 6.3
[19] *Psalm* 86.11
[20] *I Samuel* 3.9
[21] *Psalm* 22.1
[22] *Mark* 15.34
[23] I have explored this theme in *Making Good*, e.g. p. 114

Chapter 11

Speaking – Human Responsibility

Take with you words, and return to the Lord.

Hosea 14.2

Communication between people and their Maker is possible because people are enough like God. To say that is an attempt to make a more-or-less literal statement about God. It is not meant to invalidate the metaphorical statements we also make. People say that God spoke to them. They express what God said in terms of human words, formed into sentences which keep human grammatical rules. They ascribe to God lips and vocal chords. Metaphor does not have to be disreputable nor even misleading. A figure of speech can be true: 'He is eaten up with pride'. A literal statement can be false: 'Your present is just what I wanted.' Most ordinary speech is crammed with metaphor, including this present sentence; and speech about God no less.

The literal meaning of 'communicate' is 'transmit or pass on'. Human beings are social creatures. They have the capacity to communicate by transmitting their experiences to one another; and the foundation of this capacity is the characteristic human gift of language. We are speakers. It makes sense for people who picture their God as the Speaker, whose Word began everything, to look for the image of God here. Christians may be in a hurry to arrive at the point of the whole story and begin straight away to talk about love as what makes us like God: but for people to be able to love one another they must first be able to get in touch with one another. The ability to communicate is the stuff of our humanity.

It may seem a more high-powered kind of faith to leave aside the everyday sociability which is expressed in words, and concentrate devoutly on 'the flight of the alone to the Alone',[1] but this well-meaning emphasis on solitariness does not answer well to human experience, even religious experience. Our tradition, Jewish and Christian, puts a great deal of weight on the people of God, in which individuals have their roots. Life together is more basic than life apart.

Babies learn to be human from their mothers and grow up by getting to know other people. They do not start alone and then one day make the great discovery that there are other beings like themselves in the world. Social life comes first and the philosophical problem of 'our knowledge of other minds' is secondary and sophisticated. Human beings are not like polar bears or orang utans, for whom it is natural to live mostly alone. For most people, isolation is a sorrowful affliction. There are hermits; but theirs is a specialized vocation, the exception that tests the rule.

By learning to talk we enter into human life, though of course speaking is not the whole story of humanity. On the one hand, by no means all good communication is verbal. We do not always need to speak; and some of the most profound experiences go beyond words. On the other hand, by no means all good human beings are articulate. Some warm-hearted people accordingly refuse to set so much store by language and reprimand civilized society for being too 'verbal'. They reject enthusiasm about language as 'élitist', eloquence as merely talkative and precise speech as pedantic. They complain that we are a 'no touch' culture and remind us that when people are in trouble a warm hug is more comforting than persuasive arguments. This emphasis is needed, when it is identifying intellectual snobbery and redressing a false balance. It is a dire impoverishment when it becomes ingratitude for the human power of speech.

Words are our primary means of keeping in touch with other people. Peter Gärdenfors has suggested that in human evolution the social function of language may have been even more important than the passing on of information about where food is to be found. Animals bond with one another by *grooming* and the human equivalent is *gossip,* which even if it is only 'nonsensical chatter' has conspicuous advantages for our species. With language, 'you can "groom" several persons at once', and have free hands for other tasks.[2]

---

[1]　Plotinus, *Enneads*, VI. 9. 11
[2]　Gärdenfors, 2003, pp. 172–5

There is much more to language than either socializing or passing on practical information. Because words release us from the limits of the present, they endow us with a past and a future. Language relates the generations to one another as fellow human beings, the ones who are alive now, the ones who are long dead and the ones who are still to be born. Human beings comprehend their predecessors, more or less well, sometimes by their artefacts but especially by means of the words they have left behind. It is more irksome than amusing when people who want to be practical and not 'academic' assume that a scholar is 'alone in his book-lined study'. Writing is for establishing communication, a worthwhile second best for face-to-face meetings. One feels almost acquainted with David Hume on reading his defence of the dialogue form: 'the book carries us, in a manner, into company; and unites the two greatest and purest pleasures of human life, study and society'.[3]

Christians believe in the Communion of Saints, not just as a collection of people wearing haloes posed in a sort of end-of-term photograph, but as a living company. Communion is grounded in live interactions. Whatever one believes about heaven, it must allow for communication. David Jenkins offered a happy account of how he had 'begun to get glimpses, especially through other people,' that eternity would not be boring but 'could be infinitely worth it precisely because there will always be more to discover.' He had a pleasing notion, that 'one of the purposes of eternity is to be enabled by the grace of God to learn perfectly every possible language there is, so that everyone can express themselves in such a way that they will be understood fully by other people and be able to share with other people. And there, as Humpty Dumpty might say, there is glory for you. There is an eternal possibility.'[4]

A wonderful capacity necessarily gives rise to ethics. Responsible people find and live by appropriate systems of value for their variegated ways of life. Just as there are ethical standards to be applied to their professions and their business concerns, their sexual lives, their manual skills and their creative artistry, their everyday civilities and affections... so they may understand that language itself is a source of obligations. Human speech as such is a moral enterprise. It is a standing temptation to suppose that this means something negative; but a worthwhile morality will be much more than 'Thou shalt not'.

---

[3] Hume, *Dialogues Concerning Natural Religion*, Introduction
[4] Jenkins, *God, Jesus and Life in the Spirit*, 1988, pp. 38–9

It will show people what they ought to do in the positive light of what makes life worth living.

A primary duty which arises from looking on language as a human endowment is the agreeable, and therefore rather easily disregarded, duty of gratitude. Thankfulness is not fostered best by dogged determination, but by enjoyment. Moralists often need to be told to stop saying No and begin to appreciate other people, or the natural creation, or human creation. Likewise people may be better language users by pausing to enjoy the language we speak all the time. They may be pleased by its plainness, or its wit, or its beauty. They may notice the simple devices of grammar and stop taking syntax for granted. There must have once been hominids who first developed a language sophisticated enough to distinguish 'Dog bites man' from 'Man bites dog'; and 'I am hungry' both from 'I was hungry' and from 'You are hungry'. We ought to take heed of what a remarkable thing it is, that human beings can give one another information, or make one another laugh, or transport one another into the realms of gold.

People who speak the English language with its twin roots, Germanic and Latin, have special reason for gratitude that history has provided us with a multitude of words which are almost but not quite synonyms.[5] We have the choice of 'began' or 'commenced', 'careful' or 'cautious', 'pleased' or 'glad'. We can combine 'neat and tidy', 'erred and strayed', 'high and lifted up'. Without even being aware of how and when all these words arrived, we can add limitless subtlety or enrichment to our communications.

To be duly grateful for language as marvellous is more than aesthetic self-indulgence. It gives rise to the moral responsibility, which may be onerous, to look after this excellent and powerful instrument and use it properly. To take care of words is no trivial concern, but is part of the difficult and important art of taking care of one another. Whatever human skills deserve to be taken seriously, the good use of words has a high claim.

Most evidently, the good use of words requires truthfulness; but for the present that is not the main point (see below, ch. 13). Giving the first priority to truth-telling could encourage a sort of linguistic hypochondria. The ancient debate about whether and when it is permissible to tell a lie is naturally concerned with negative arguments, a matter of prohibitions and permissions. These could be a distraction from attending to the positive moral responsibilities of

[5]   Bragg, *The Adventure of English*, 2003

language-using creatures. The basic purpose of speech, whether primitive or sophisticated, is to get ideas 'as exactly as possible out of one mind into another.'[6] The first concern of the ethics of language should be the responsibility of each generation to cherish this wonderful precision tool.

Unfortunately it is not true that 'we needs must love the highest when we see it'.[7] Often 'bad money drives out good'. Trivial examples are not too foolish to be pointed out, when what is at stake is indeed the trivializing of an excellent human capacity. Some preachers can hardly say 'we live' without adding 'and move and have our being'.[8] A 'change' is apt to be a 'sea change', whether it has happened on dry land or not. It appears hard to assert merely that two phenomena are linked: they have to be linked 'inextricably', simply because 'linked' and 'inextricably' themselves have become inextricably linked. So language makes whatever happens look fated.

Do these compulsions matter? It is not priggish to insist on the importance of people thinking what they say. Linguistic free-wheeling leads to inconvenience. Even when there is no doubt about what is meant, it matters that the process of understanding one another should be dreary and arduous when it could be life-enhancing and enlightening.

There is no need for gloom. Later editions of *Plain Words*, a handbook for civil servants, were able to take some unpleasing infelicities out. It is instructive and not altogether depressing to look at A.P. Herbert's *What a Word*, published in 1935. He set up an 'Entrance examination for words seeking admission to the English language' and awarded marks out of ten under four headings: Understood? Can we admire you? Are you good (i.e. correctly formed)? Do we require you? He wanted to reject, for example, 'motivate', 'recondition', 'hospitalize'; but he accepted 'television' as understood and needed, though neither beautiful nor well-formed. He had some success, including scotching 'inst., ult. and prox'. It is probably forgotten now that what we call a 'green belt' was beginning to be called a 'sterile area'.

The enemy is not novelty. It is language which takes control of its speakers instead of giving them control. Language cannot be kept static and ought not to be kept static, even if people deplore some of

[6]   G.M. Young, quoted in Gowers *Plain Words*, 1954
[7]   Tennyson, *Idylls of the King*, 'Guinevere'
[8]   See *Acts* 17.28

its developments. Although we 'speak the tongue that Shakespeare spake', the word 'spake' itself is a reminder that we do not even speak the tongue that Wordsworth spoke. The constant awareness that language is always growing is the very reason why it needs to be cherished.

Language is made by speakers and writers, not by grammarians or schoolteachers. Nor is it made, as Dr Johnson knew, by dictionary-compilers: 'who do not form, but register the language; who do not teach men how they should think, but relate how they have hitherto expressed their thoughts'.[9] He could not know that two hundred and fifty years later his dictionary, still in print, would be expected to instruct 'people' rather than 'men'.

When language is altering, the criterion for acceptance is certainly not whether an expression is new, nor even whether it is quite logi-cal, but whether it is a help or a hindrance in saying what we mean. That is what is wrong with using 'alibi' to mean not 'elsewhere' but 'excuse'; and with using 'disinterested' to mean 'uninterested'. As usual, example is more use than precept. It is not much good to say 'That's wrong': but it may help to say 'That's inefficient', and show why. This new expression is misleadingly inaccurate; that one blurs a useful distinction. On the other hand, there are good developments as well as bad. For instance, the ancient word 'hospice' has been revived lately to fill a newly-understood need. Computer language is often vivid and telling, because it is shaped by people who know what they are doing rather than wandered into by people who do not care.

Meanwhile the latest cliché arrives and departs. 'The flavour of the month' is the flavour of the month. 'Watchdogs' take a sur-prisingly active part in political life. They are more likely to be 'set up' or to be 'appalled' than to bark. When people fail to picture what they are saying, they are inclined to 'wrestle with competing frameworks' or find 'concrete life in a grassroots framework.' 'Concrete' indeed is a rich source of nonsense: 'The idea took flight and became a concrete proposal.' There is much potential amuse-ment in mixed metaphors: 'He is a snake in the ointment.'[10]

The habit of critical attention to language as people use it can be entertaining and does not have to be unkind, destructive, or obscu-rantist. It might even have something to do with being a good lis-tener. To take notice of how words and sentences are put together

[9]   Johnson, Preface to *A Dictionary of the English Language*, 1755
[10] I believe that all these examples are genuine.

and the effects they create is a good way of realising appreciatively
what a remarkable power human speech is.

There is more to the ethics of language than taking care that our
words shall accurately mirror the world. Living creatures are more
than cameras recording their surroundings: they are agents. People
do things with words. We often play with words, but still more often
we work with them. Words are dynamic. 'I will' marries a man and a
woman. 'I promise' is a commitment, not merely a forecast. 'Present
arms' does more than report that this is going to happen next: it gives
the order which makes it happen. As philosophers put it, these are
'performative' utterances.[11] Speaking is one main kind of human
doing.

The words people use are not morally neutral inert tokens.
Because they are powerful, they can hurt. One of the greatest obsta-
cles to human understanding, let alone Christian love, is the human
tendency to think in stereotypes. Words like 'posh', 'yob', 'femi-
nine', 'queer', 'ethnic', 'primitive', 'wealthy', 'trendy' express pre-
conceived notions about class, gender, race, life-style. Natural as
they are, these shortcuts are a menace, when they hinder people
from seeing one another as real. It is easy to put a label on something
and then hard to unstick it. It is no use to say that 'academic' really
means 'to do with an academy', now that it has moved, by way of the
fairly neutral 'theoretical', to the antagonistic 'impractical, irrelevant', and has thereby become a stick for beating scholars.

Taking care of language is not mere 'political correctness', but
charity. Saying 'men' when one means 'people' is not even actually
incorrect, unlike saying 'I refute that' instead of 'I deny that'. Until
recently it has been entirely correct English to use 'men' for 'men and
women' and 'he' for 'he or she'. Unfortunately this idiosyncrasy of
our language, once convenient, has become increasingly misleading
and has done a good deal of harm. It is an inefficient usage which has
allowed generations of human beings to forget that women are people too.

If only it were true that 'man' and 'he' were really inclusive and
need not mislead anyone. People argue that it is entirely reasonable
simply to say 'man'. 'Man' is the proper translation for 'homo', and
'homo' means inclusively 'human being'. Only when 'man' trans-
lates 'vir' must it mean 'male'. Convenient as this would be, it needs
to be tested. Would anyone ever say 'She is a good man', meaning 'a
good human being?' Might 'This was a great man' mean Elizabeth

[11]   Austin, *How to do Things with Words*, 1962

Fry or Florence Nightingale? That is not the way our language has developed. If someone says 'There's a man in the room', he will not turn out to be a woman in the way that 'I saw the doctor' is nowadays just as likely to mean a woman doctor. 'Manhood' calls up a picture of 'manly' qualities not of humane qualities. When people say 'man' they are still understood to mean specifically *vir*, male person, not generally *homo sapiens*.

Many people of goodwill think that concern with inclusive language is much ado about nothing much. They need to be convinced that to change our ways of speaking has become a moral obligation. There is still resistance, not only from people who are convinced that after all men really are superior to women, but from people who cannot be bothered. They can see for themselves that a great deal of 'politically correct' language is tiresome, and are happy to proceed no further. So, as usual, the moderates, who realise that fairness demands hard work, are squeezed between the extremists who have already taken sides.

Chapter 12
Thinking

Sure he that made us with such large discourse,
Looking before and after, gave us not
That capability and god-like reason
To fust in us unused.

Hamlet, IV. 4

There are plenty of possible ways of specifying what it means to be human, some more flattering than others. We are rational animals, hairless bipeds, children of God, miserable sinners, creative artists, social animals, pairbonding animals, animals who go to war with our own kind. Many of our particular capacities require us to excel at imitation.[1] We can do so many different things because we are adaptable opportunist animals 'We are not innately *anything*', declared Richard Leakey.[2]

It is more sensible to look for *characteristic* rather than *unique* accomplishments of humanity, celebrating rather than stipulating. The argument about continuity and discontinuity must go both ways. On the one hand, human beings have more in common with other animals, at least with other mammals, than they may suppose. Apes make tools for poking by stripping the leaves from sticks. In captivity they have been taught to use language.[3] Dogs evidently understand human words. Geese are monogamous and mourn their mates. Kittens play. Chimpanzees greet rushing water with an apparently ritual dance.[4]

And yet, on the other hand, it made sense for George Herbert to call attention to human distinctiveness:

---

[1]   See *Encyclopaedia Britannica,* Vol. 8 'Hominidae' p. 1027; Liebermann, *Uniquely Human,* 1991, pp. 140–1.
[2]   Leakey, *The Making of Mankind,* 1981, p. 242; *Encyclopaedia Britannica,* Vol. 8 'Homo erectus' p. 1034
[3]   See above, pp. 77–8 and note 5 there
[4]   See p. 129 below and note 7 there

Nothing wears clothes, but Man; nothing doth need
But he to wear them. Nothing useth fire,
But Man alone.[5]

Only human beings carry things about in containers,[6] use tools to make tools,[7] express their thoughts in writing, paint portraits, do sums, travel to the moon, invite one another to dinner, want to know their own history, arrange celebrations, worship God. Though humble gratitude for the glory of the whole universe may prompt us to play down human uniqueness, it is just as seemly to be grateful for the particular wonder of the creatures we are.

The time has come to give *reason* its due. The ancient conviction that 'Man' is the *rational* animal is not the whole story, but it is an element of the story. Human powers of reason are a fundamental part of the belief that human beings are made in God's image. Describing what sort of creature *homo sapiens* is without mentioning intelligence would be like describing birds without mentioning their wings. We are perfectly aware that there are flightless birds, like ostriches, and that there are other creatures who fly, like bees and bats; but still if we are classifying species, 'flying creature' is a convenient category for birds.

Likewise 'rational creatures' is indeed a convenient category for human beings, even though being reasonable is neither a necessary nor a sufficient condition of being human. It is a false step to make a stand on one single ground of our uniqueness, '*the* difference between man and beast'. Rather than arguing legalistically that reason is the essential qualification for being children of God, we ought rather to appreciate it gratefully, as a characteristic excellence of our species.

The glory of human reason depends upon the glory of language. It is by learning to talk that babies learn to think. A small child mastering a language is achieving a marvel, taking a huge step into the heritage of humankind, which bears comparison with the great steps into new intellectual worlds made by Newton and Einstein. Human beings, of all creatures, have the capacity to transcend the present moment by 'thinking in absence'. They make language the bridge between their own experience and everything else.

Austin Farrer identified 'that special likeness to God, which men have above the beasts' as 'the power to get outside our skins, and see

[5]   Herbert, *Works*, 'Providence' in 'The Church' p. 120
[6]   Leakey & Lewin, 1977, pp. 116, 162
[7]   Eliade, *A History of Religious Ideas*, 1978, Vol. I, p. 3

things impartially'. Much follows from this, if only one can keep one's head and not get distracted by 'men', which in the twenty-first century might seem to dismiss women and beasts alike. Farrer was sure that all creatures are God's handiwork. He looked at real birds in his garden who were feeding their young and singing, and enjoyed their capacity for altruism and even artistry. 'I do not say that thrush over there is a Bach or a Mozart, but how can I doubt that the song he sings is poured from the well of pure delight, or how can I deny the skill with which he turns and voices his phrase?'

That was the setting, more like the world of Wordsworth than of Descartes, in which Austin Farrer praised God for the special distinction 'of man alone, that God made him in his own image, after his very likeness'. The special human gift he is identifying is the rational capacity to 'see with God's impartial eyes, to see our own bodies crowding among the other bodies on the earth'. This capacity is by no means simply intellectual. The context in which Farrer placed it was a sermon entitled 'The generous eye.' What gives 'a touch of the divine' to this ability of human beings to transcend themselves is not a matter of brainpower, but of recognizing the ethical demand to take more than just ourselves into account.[8]

Like many others, Austin Farrer wrote in a way which would now be called 'speciesist'. He did not appear anxious about asserting that 'the rational person offers an opening to God's mercy which humbler creatures do not'.[9] 'It is right', he went on, 'that brutes should take their chance … But the rational person God specially saves.' He is plainly using 'rational' to mean something more important than the sort of fiddly ratiocination which does sums with ideas. He may none the less be at some risk of encouraging people to think of God, the Creator of the rational person, as an intellectual snob. It is hard nowadays to praise human reason without inviting an accusation of human arrogance.

It would be satisfactory to put aside the notion that the Almighty has a kind of option for the clever. Unfortunately, in reaction, the next step may be to convert us in God's name into inverted intellectual snobs. From celebrating intelligence, are we now to say that it is not a great gift after all? If it is just as good to be a 'dumb beast' as a rational animal, does that mean acknowledging, if we really want to get rid of 'speciesism', that a just God counts us indeed on all fours with the animals? Instead of glorying in our faith that our Creator

---

[8]   Farrer, *The End of Man*, 1973, p. 21–2
[9]   Farrer, 1966, p. 107

chose to become a man rather than any other creature, we might be ashamed. Was it because innocent animals did not need a Redeemer that God the Son took human flesh?

The response must be, once again, to say both/and. Human beings are sinful and yet are still be counted as a special kind of animal, in somewhat the same way as the children of Israel could be sinful and still be God's chosen people. If one believes that Israel was chosen to have a particular role among the nations, one may believe that humanity has a particular role among God's creatures. Christians affirm that God's communication with Israel has been for the sake of all humanity. We may hope that God's restoration of humanity likewise is not to stop with humanity but is to include the whole of creation. The story that Adam, still unfallen, was given the task of naming the animals can be put alongside St Paul's evocative thought that the reconciliation of fallen humanity is to be part of the reconciliation of the whole creation, 'groaning in travail together until now'.[10] C.F.D. Moule described that passage in the Epistle to the Romans as 'the most remarkable statement in the whole New Testament about the relation of man to nature'.[11]

As a matter of justice, we ought to take the trouble now to substitute 'humanity' for 'man', though it is bound to be daunting for people who value their heritage of thinking and poetry expressed in English words.

> Men (and women?) are we, and must grieve when even the Shade
> Of that which once was great is passed away.[12]

Political correctness has no right to tinker with Wordsworth's terminology, but historical commonsense can take hold of what he meant, refuse to be distracted and continue to admire his poem. What is required is not to jettison or belittle our tradition, but to make the necessary effort to convey today's thoughts sensitively.

It is a still more exacting endeavour to look at the matter as well as the manner of today's thoughts. We cannot avoid attending to the ancient question 'What is man?' because, however we express it, it needs answering more than ever. Being made in God's image and likeness makes more complicated demands than looking reverently towards the Creator. The question what human life means includes the challenging substantive task of also looking towards the world of nature and identifying human beings as rational *animals*. What

---

[10]   *Romans* 8.19-23; see also *Colossians* 1.20
[11]   Moule, 'Man and Nature in the New Testament', 1964.
[12]   Wordsworth, Sonnet 'On the extinction of the Venetian Republic'

this requires, yet again, is both/and: to hold together *both* the distinctive and truly godlike character of human reason, *and* the diversity of gifts and needs shared with the other animals.

To comprehend what kind of particular gift human rationality is, it should help to pick up Gilbert Ryle's discussion of 'Thought that is peculiar to the human animal' (see above p. 31). It is not just intellect which he is emphasizing as distinctively human, but a more far-reaching capability which includes struggling to get things right and sometimes getting them wrong. What he meant by 'Thought' includes ratiocination, but is more fundamental. A favourite expression of his was 'using our wits.'

Understanding is an inclusive way of identifying this kind of intelligence, which can betoken a whole range of gifts from wisdom to mental agility. The scope of human reason extends all the way from simple comprehension, by way of lucid analysis and inspired insight, to the wisdom of Solomon. The more precise idea of *discernment* applies usefully to the whole range. The 'understanding heart' which the king asked for in his dream and which was granted to him is made more plain by the newer translation a 'discerning mind'.[13] The example the story immediately goes on to give is his benevolent ingenuity in discovering which of two women was the mother of the live baby and which was lying.

It is worth reiterating that Ryle's more open 'hospitable' way of thinking about Thought, as especially characteristic of human beings, is not a matter of having, or of not having, a 'soul'. A thinking creature might be spiritual or secular. To assert that only human beings have souls, whether that is true or not, is not the same as to say that only human beings are rational, whether that is true or not.

Rationality in Ryle's way of explaining it may be well compared with physical prowess. Each of these is a characteristic endowment of humanity which it is a disablement to lack; which is wonderful if it is present in any degree; and which is sometimes present in a specially high degree which calls for admiration, or even in a superlative degree which calls for wonder. To be the first to run a mile in four minutes or to discover the theory of relativity may be comparable though incommensurable achievements, calling for due celebration.

A main meaning of human rationality is that human beings want to find out what the world is like. Pigs root out truffles, and dogs hide bones and later dig them up. People too are capable of digging

[13]   *I Kings* 3.5–14

in the earth and finding what may be hidden there; but their characteristic discoveries come from pondering and wondering. When
they dirty their hands, they are often also busy thinking out what
they are doing.

Pondering is an example of what Austin Farrer called 'getting outside our skins'. Wondering begins with simple puzzlement, when
people ask themselves and one another for explanations. 'I wonder
why she is looking so distracted.' 'I wonder why apples fall down
not up.' Wondering about *why* people and things behave as they do
may lead on to wondering *at* their complexity or their beauty and
eventually to feeling wonder in the sense in which it means something like awe.

Finding out what the world is like may be no more than casual
curiosity, innocent or maybe intrusive; but its characteristic setting is
the responsiveness of well-taught pupils, the alertness of enquiring
minds, the courage of explorers and the job-satisfaction, indeed the
vocation, of research scientists. For all these, accuracy matters, getting the facts right. 'Never mind: that will do' will not do.

Christianity has much to say about Truth and the church has fostered many learned lives. Unfortunately it is also a conspicuous part
of the indictment against religion brought by sceptical humanists,
that orthodoxy has too often treated enquiry into the physical nature
of God's creation as self-indulgent or irreverent. Augustine and
Aquinas could be saints, using their reason to the glory of God, but
Galileo was repudiated and Darwin was deplored.

The 'capability and god-like reason' characteristic of the human
animal is practical as much as theoretical. Part of the meaning of
'looking before and after' is exercising forethought, having policies
and carrying them out. There are many arguments about how
non-human creatures do or do not come into this picture.[14] What
does it mean to call an animal intelligent? Do animals have beliefs?
Do they make plans? Do they have life stories of their own?

People write biographies of animals, imaginary or real. Anna
Sewell depicted the sufferings and joys of Black Beauty the Victorian
carriage-horse. Virginia Woolf wrote the life of Elizabeth Barrett
Browning's dog Flash. The story of Jambo, the silverback gorilla at
Gerald Durrell's zoo, was written by his keeper.[15] Whether one
warms to these narratives, or disdains them for their human point of
view, one would never expect them to be *auto*biographies. Animal

---

[14]   See Regan, 2004, ch. 2
[15]   Johnstone-Scott, *Jambo*, 1995

life stories are both unlike and like human life stories. On the one hand, they have to be written, read and criticized by human beings, not by the subjects of the stories. On the other hand, they are not fable or fantasy, unlike the Tales of Beatrix Potter, whose delicately-drawn convincing dressed-up country creatures have entered into the imaginations of many children and still delight the grown-ups they once were. A narrative of the natural life lived by an animal, wild or tame, claims to give a realistic account of what animal existence is like, true as a matter of fact, or convincingly true to life in the same way as a novel is convincing.

To think of many animals as being rational enough to have purposes, and of some as having biographies, is common sense, not sentimental anthropomorphism. Most of us are sure that animals are not automata. We cannot deny that their feelings, wants, hopes and efforts are what they seem to be. That is what is meant by the belief that an animal is 'the subject of a life',[16] which is taken as the foundation of animal rights or at least of human duties to animals.

But still most of us cannot believe that this amounts to Hamlet's 'large discourse, looking before and after'. There is a stage beyond having a life story. The human *thinking* which is pondering and wondering means more than being aware of good or bad experiences. Thinking even goes further than the rational ability, which many animals surely have, to make plans and carry them out. Beyond the passive awareness of what is going on, and beyond the conscious behaviour which sets about altering what is going on, there is the self-awareness which is conscious of being conscious: whether this is counted as a difference of degree or a difference of kind. Being a creature with a life story, who does things successfully or unsuccessfully and is pleased or sorry, may not mean perceiving one's own self as a living subject. Human beings are creatures who not only have life stories but know that they are individuals and call themselves 'I'.

There is a further stage yet of rationality beyond knowing who one is, which is having a world picture. People place their life stories in contexts beyond their own experience and hold beliefs about what the universe is like. They find out not only what is the case, but why. They analyse concepts and proceed to develop philosophies. Plato was rational in a way gorillas never are.

To rush into saying so much might be thoughtless. One could easily slip into both 'speciesism' about animals and also 'élitism' about human beings. Plato was hardly a typical man. If he is set up as *man*

[16]   Regan, 2004

the philosopher, in plain contrast to the beasts that have no understanding, most of humanity will hardly count as rational. It will not
do to put forward as the foremost human excellence a capability
which only a few human beings share. Humanity is more interest-
ingly diverse than that.

Yet reason is still glorious and still characteristic of humankind,
and having a world picture is part of what we mean by being rational. This human capability does not have to be so narrow that only
the specialized manifestation of reasoning which is philosophizing
would be allowed to count. A world view need not be sophisticated.
As well as abstract philosophical theories which many people cannot comprehend, there are 'philosophies of life', and attitudes to life,
on which people take their stand. People announce the ways they
understand the world by declaring, 'What I always say is' as much as
by saying 'Human life is solitary, poor, nasty, brutish and short',[17] or
'The starry heaven above me and the moral law within me',[18] or 'In
the beginning was the Word'.[19]

There still need be no sharp cut-off point between distinct
worked-out world views and unselfconscious outlooks. The cheer-
fulness or grumpiness, caution or confidence which characterize
individual human beings are ways of seeing the world which may
have little to do with mental processes. The variegated dispositions
of particular animals might find a place on this spectrum, even
though they do not have to be put under the heading of 'reason'.

[17]   Hobbes, *Leviathan*, 1651, 1.13
[18]   Kant, *Critique of Practical Reason*, Conclusion
[19]   *John* 1.1

Chapter 13

Telling

God uses us to help each other so.
Lending our minds out

Robert Browning, 'Fra Lippo Lippi'

One could presumably have a world view of one's very own, but
most people share their ideas and develop them together. If thinking
about the importance of human reason led me to suppose that cogi-
tating all by myself is basic or even likely, it would be time to get the
argument back on track. Human beings do not set off as solipsists or
even as polar bears (see above p. 84). They live their lives, including
their mental lives, in company. They find out most of what they
know by making their thoughts available to one another, telling and
being told. 'It is astonishing what foolish things one can temporarily
believe if one thinks too long alone' remarked J.M. Keynes in the
Preface to his monumental book on economic theory.[1]

The rational human enterprise of finding out what the world is
like, in elementary or profound ways, is characteristically a co-oper-
ative pursuit: pursuit in both its senses, occupation and chase. People pursue careers and they pursue quarries. In all their pursuits,
collaboration is as important as competition. People show one
another things, large and small, practical and theoretical, what has
happened to them and what they have found out.[2] Keeping in touch
is necessary for human flourishing.

Of course communication is no human monopoly. The complex
and diverse ways by which animals communicate may be compared
and contrasted with human language. Mammals in particular bring
up infants, enjoy company and pass on information. On the other
hand, even our near relatives the apes do not instinctively show one

---

[1]   Keynes, *The General Theory of Employment, Interest and Money*, 1936, p. xxiii
[2]   Oppenheimer, 2001, ch. 17

another things by pointing,[3] they do not find words of their own, nor give other creatures names, and they do not study.

Human children, like other young animals and even more so, have to be educated before they can take their places in the grown-up world. In human life, learning from other people is by no means reserved for children. Telling each other is lifelong. This present book, which is exploring what human beings are by putting thoughts into words to show to other people, might be called an illustration of its own subject-matter.

What people need if they are to be capable of learning is not immaturity but honesty. Even a lone student, responsible to nobody else, would be lost without the integrity to grasp the difference between certainty and conjecture, hypothesis and proof, knowledge and taking for granted. Members of the human community who work together and depend upon each other carry the responsibilities of their common life. They need to rely fully on knowing that they can generally believe other people, in the same way as they can generally trust that the laws of nature will hold. Stones do not fall upwards, pigs do not fly and the statements people make are not usually false. The famous riddle about the explorer who encounters one tribe who always tell the truth and another tribe who always tell lies, and has to find out what he needs to know by asking the right question, is a test of logic not a report on anthropology. For human life to be even possible, let alone agreeable, honesty must be the norm and deceit must be parasitic upon truthfulness.

But how much truthfulness do human beings need? How general is 'generally'? Discussion of the ethics of truth-telling was set aside earlier as distracting.[4] The marvellous endowment of language deserved positive appreciation first, without legalistic arguments about whether and when language may be used to say what is not true. But now the question about the wrongness of lying is relevant, for giving honesty its rightful place in human life.[5] Understanding what human beings are includes understanding their need for reliable communication, their dependence on telling and being told.

We do not doubt that lying is wrong, but the question what counts as a lie may not be easy to answer. Lying is not always a matter of saying something false; and deception does not even have to be linguistic. Some animals are capable of deceit. A mother bird who

---

[3]   Gärdenfors, 2003, pp. 123–4
[4]   Above p. 86
[5]   Oppenheimer, 'The truth-telling animal', 2000

instinctively lures a predator away from her nest by pretending to have an injured wing[6] is not exactly a liar but she is achieving a liar's purposes. Human beings too can deceive without words, sending out false signals with the innocent or guilty intention of giving misleading information. Is tinted hair a lie? Is it untruthful to arrange for the lights in my house to be lit when I am out? It is surely telling a lie to sell an inferior product which has been silently substituted for the real thing, even if nothing has been said.

The essential human duty of honesty is not always a plain matter of knowing what lies are, knowing that lies are wrong and resisting the temptation to tell them. Most of us think that there are circumstances in which to deceive somebody is even the right thing to do. The stock example is misdirecting a dangerous enemy. Casuists would say: 'In this case a false statement is not a *lie*, in the same way as justifiable homicide is not murder. Go ahead and say, "He went that way" and don't feel guilty.' Others would reach the same result by a different route: 'Saying what is not true is *always* lying but some lies are not wrong.' Rigorists would still insist: 'Lying is always wrong. Just tell the truth and your conscience will be clear, even if the results are horrible.' Various inviting paths lead in different directions around this confrontation and the chance of getting morally lost is high.

Even careful and sincere questioning about what counts as lying and what makes deceit wrong, or sometimes not wrong, what rules can safely be applied, may not lead reliably to good communication. Finding one's way through the thicket needs a different way in, by way of understanding what truth-telling is for. The context of communication is community. As language users we need openness and truthfulness, because we live in one world and it is a nightmare if we cannot trust one another. That is why it is safest to start with the assumption that truth must be told. A lie, however desirable its immediate consequences, damages the foundation of good faith on which human society depends. So mitigating circumstances may not make the lie *right*. Instead they may allow it to be deemed forgivable and even to be the least of evils.

Little white lies are supposed to be obviously forgivable but they may do more harm to human communication than big black ones. 'I like your dress' is socially acceptable but spreads the kind of foggy unreliability which makes everyday trust impossible. 'I never stole that dress' is a plain example of a deplorable lie but there is no

---

[6] Uhlenbroek, 2002, p. 238

human relationship here for it to undermine. It is just what a thief would say and we already know that unfortunately some people are thieves. When the problem is posed in this way, that what is wrong with untruthfulness is that it poisons the atmosphere, it becomes less tempting to adopt a kindly liberal point of view which tolerates all manner of lies because strict truth-telling is harsh. For the sake of our common life, there is a lot to be said in favour of a presumption for truthfulness, even in small matters.[7]

It might be, as lawyers put it, a rebuttable presumption. People who threaten, and even people who pry, have surely lost their place in our common life and forfeited their ordinary right to be told the truth. Bandits, unscrupulous journalists and inquisitive acquaintances ought not to assume that they can count upon their victims' honesty. It would be priggish, not noble, to insist on telling them the truth.

More surprisingly, there is a case to be made for equivocation. Uttering precisely true statements with the intention to deceive certainly looks like a tricky and legalistic way of not being in the wrong, but it may have a kind of integrity, dangerous but defensible. People have a right to defend their privacy against intrusion. More than that, they have the duty to keep other people's secrets. If they refuse to speak, that will give away immediately that there is something to hide. To equivocate may be the most honest way someone can devise to refrain from giving an answer. If I take full responsibility for my words being reliable as far as they go, I can be allowed to hope that you will not notice what I have not said. You can trust me at least not to put any poison into the system, which is better than trusting my fallible judgment that *this* much poison is little enough to be harmless.

If we could get rid of the idea that white lies are quite all right, we might try harder to put a firm presumption for truthfulness into practice. 'Truth' said John Austin Baker, 'is an ardent and exhilarating virtue'. That should not make it any less practical. Instead of endowing Truth with a kind of mental capital T which removes it from everyday life, it should be feasible to set about teaching children that putting temptations to lie in each other's way is wrong. They are taught that it is wrong to put temptations to steal in people's way by leaving one's property around. Likewise it should be a matter of ordinary morality that it is wrong to tempt people to lie by asking questions to which one has no right to an answer. The embar-

[7]   Baker, *The Foolishness of God*, 1970, pp. 89–90

rassment of being interrogated is not always a trivial kind of hurt. If people are to be expected not to lie nor even equivocate, they badly need the protection of 'a greater liberty to keep silent'[8] than they have at present.

Elementary truthfulness about what is going on is the needful foundation on which human communication can be built. When this basis is firm, there is much more for people to understand and tell to one another than their immediate ordinary experience. There is exploring to be done. People need to know who they are, where they have come from and where they are going. They want to tell their life stories and they are apt to go on looking further, into past history, into physics, into metaphysics. For many people, having a world view is not a luxury. Another possible characterization of human beings might be 'world-view-forming' creatures.

Because we are social animals who explore the world and the universe together, who depend upon one another's support in nourishing our minds as much as in nourishing our bodies, our world views need to stay grounded in the 'common or garden' reality of shared social life. There is a trap easy to fall into, first to agree indeed that good communication depends upon truth, then to recognize that there are different kinds of truth, and then to go on to apply the ethics of truthfulness only to the humbler kinds of truth. Then the higher levels of human thought are somehow raised above down-to-earth factual reality and do not have to be taken so literally.

Believing as we do that we are a special kind of animal, we may be tempted to presume upon our 'right to roam' in these higher levels. We are human creatures endowed with language. We have learnt to talk; and we go on to put our animal origins further behind us and learn to talk about matters beyond common sense. We still need to hold on to some connection between truthful communication and what is the case. When people make a religious statement like 'God created the universe' are they saying that something happened; or if not, what are they saying? In the rarefied air of those lofty regions, it takes a brave kind of naivety to maintain that what makes a statement true not false still has something to do with whether it corresponds with matter of fact.

A 'correspondence theory' of truth comes naturally to plain thinkers; but philosophers, poets and even theologians are apt to brush such a simple notion aside as naïve; and not only naïve but insensitive and intolerant towards other people. Liberal-mined thinkers

---

[8]   Baker, 1970, pp. 89–90

have lost confidence that statements about inaccessible realities need to claim to be *true*. They are afraid of taking sides which they do not at all want to take, and aligning themselves with bigotry. The word 'nuanced' is in favour. To hanker after yes-or-no objective facts looks like fundamentalism; and fundamentalism connotes fanaticism and even terrorism.

If people accordingly loosen their grip upon the notion that proper thinking must be a matter of fact-finding, they still, like any living creature, remain fact-bound. Reality can come and hit them: if it cannot, it is not reality. The elementary questions which we all ask one another to find out what is true take the form, What happened? What is going on? Whatever next? Answers to these questions give information, reliable or unreliable, about truths which are not for us to invent.

What makes such simple confidence controversial is the awareness that answers may not be available. People who mind about truth must come to terms somehow with the risk that facts beyond immediate human experience may turn out to be beyond our reach and maybe beyond our reach in principle. No wonder it seems attractive then to say that these are not real facts, to stop worrying about taking our world views so literally and to settle for other kinds of truth which do not have to be set against falsity. What is wrong with this would-be encouraging policy is the principle announced by the logical positivists, that statements which run no risk of being false cannot mean enough to say anything in particular.[9]

People's world views, and especially their religious beliefs, cannot be kept isolated from the ways human beings characteristically make discoveries by communication with one another. Christian people in particular should take this warning to heart, because their faith is tied up, more than many world views, with information. The beliefs they hold about how things are have been reported to them as true by other human beings. No doubt a good deal more humble agnosticism would be appropriate; and a good deal more sensitivity to the understanding that some things we cannot know, and some things cannot well be expressed literally. It is still futile to expect that a faith to live by could reside inaccessibly in one's own head or one's own heart, floating free of beliefs shared with other people.

---

[9]   Ayer, *Language, Truth and Logic*, 1936

Chapter 14

Making

And the glorious majesty of the Lord our God be upon us:
prosper thou the work of our hands upon us,
O prosper thou our handiwork.

Psalm 90.17

At all levels, practical and theoretical, from everyday administration
to metaphysical theory or to divine worship, it matters a great deal to
human beings to share their lives. They recount to one another their
life stories, 'looking before and after'. They ask each other for news
about their present doings and their future hopes and plans. They
reminisce about the past. 'The first time we met, you were wearing a
bright pink dress.' 'He'll remember with advantages what feats he
did that day'.[1] 'Let us now praise famous men, and our fathers that
begat us'.[2] Even firm sceptics, who are convinced that we really
know very little, do not aspire to live entirely in the present. They
mind about what is going to happen; and in everyday life they take
heed, not only for themselves, but for their descendants when they
will have gone.

As people become more sophisticated, the narratives they recount
about olden days consolidate into chronicles; and chronicles become
sources for history. One form which the duty of truthfulness takes,
sooner or later, is an obligation to distinguish legend from objective
fact. Sometimes people tell entertaining or enlightening tales and
sometimes they interpret evidence, and both these are characteristic
and life-enhancing human activities; but one needs to understand
the difference.

The huge question of myth and what it may mean to call a myth
true looms up forthwith and may confuse the issue. Myths are one
example of the human tendency to communicate with one another
by way of narrative. How particular myths arose, and whether any

---

[1]   *Henry V*, IV. 3. 50–1
[2]   *Ecclesiasticus* 44.1

individual human beings were responsible for their creation and development, is not something we can now discover. Pandora opening her box and Eve taking the serpent's advice are both narratives about how the troubles of the world began. Whatever the people who first told these stories believed, it is hardly obligatory nowadays to take either as prosaic history. We can still find either or both illuminating, or childish, or profound, or sexist, or true to life, or indeed inspired. Christian theologians, traditional and radical, have much to say and many questions to ask about what role myths ought to have in faith; how far the affirmations of the Creeds are, or are not, 'mythical'; and whether if they are mythical they are any less true.

The present enquiry is not about myths and how they may contribute to theological understanding. The question is rather to consider and try to illuminate what human creatures are. When we have come to think of ourselves as essentially communicators, to fit our characteristic activity of story-telling into place is a good way forward. Both factual reporting and creative invention are human aptitudes, belonging to our gift of thinking in absence.[3] These skills evidently exceed anything we ascribe to any other animal, but can still be seen as growing out of their roots in our animal ancestry.

People who like the idea that 'man' was created as the *rational* animal may happily recognize the role of coherent narrative for telling one another about how things are. They may acknowledge, gladly or grudgingly, that other creatures are capable of imparting information. The next step is to understand that this divine ability extends beyond such prosaic bounds. Charlotte Uhlenbroek points out that 'Both animals and humans often put a lot more time and energy into communication than is strictly necessary to get information across'.[4] The way creatures reflect the glory of their Creator is revealed not only in their ability to handle given facts, but in the creative capacities of finite beings.

Wordsworth's green linnet presiding over 'the revels of the May', Austin Farrer's thrush who poured his song 'from the well of pure delight',[5] are literally music-makers and metaphorically artists. It is hard to say whether it is literal or metaphorical to identify real enjoyment here, a first step towards the elation a human creator feels when a piece of work 'comes right.' It is not whimsical to suggest that these are examples of a dimension of worthwhileness which is

---

[3]   See above, pp. 79, 92
[4]   Uhlenbroek, 2002, p. 246
[5]   Above, p. 93

more than practical convenience. Beyond intelligence there is inspiration, coming to fruition in humankind.

It would be surprising if the 'image of God' had nothing to do with imagination.[6] *Homo faber*, 'man the maker', is broad enough to be one of the better definitions of humanity. It includes making by hand and word, shaping clay into pots and ideas into poems, constructing buildings and arguments, composing melodies, depicting and devising. Kipling's ship's engineer McAndrew could not help exulting in the glory of his steam engines,

> ... singin' like the Morning Stars for joy that they are made ...
> Uplift am I? When first in store the new-made beasties stood,
> Were Ye cast down that breathed the Word declarin' all things good?

There is a world of inspired activity in which people may well be called sub-creators. They behave as God's creatures by imitating, indeed *imaging*, their Creator, by bringing something new into the world. God indeed can create *ex nihilo*, from nothing; but human beings, like their Maker, can make something which is more than its given ingredients. Not only can people *think* in absence, reasoning about things which do not need to be present here and now. They can set about creatively inventing new combinations of ideas which so far are not present anywhere.

Creative thinking goes back as far as human beings go back. The first hominid who bashed sharp-edged flakes off a flint was no less an innovator than Alexander Bell who invented the telephone. There is no reason why the story cannot go further back still, without any exclusive cut-off point for defining humanity. The advances of human stone-age technology may in their turn be examples of the same kind of inspiration as the ingenuity of the first ape who stripped the leaves off a stick to poke grubs out of a hole. The 'tool-making animal' can still be splendid without being unique.

We are in the world of 'both/and', gradually taken over by 'compare and contrast'. Animals appear to enjoy exercising their physical prowess in something like the way energetic human beings do. Some animals visibly apply themselves to solving problems and are evidently in some sense pleased when they succeed. People who work with animals are not sentimental, and need not be anthropomorphic, when they marvel at their individual achievements as they might marvel at the achievements of human beings.

---

[6]   The argument of this chapter is part résumé, part development of the chapter called 'Making' in Oppenheimer, 2001.

Of course there is a vast difference between the endeavour of a bird who instinctively builds an elaborate nest and the plans of a student who enrols at a college of architecture. Must we see nothing but contrast and admit no continuity, or might these enterprises both be manifestations of natural creativity? It would be misplaced loyalty to our own species to deny flatly that both sorts of effort might find a place on one spectrum.

And yet … it would be just as obstinate a prejudice to see nothing distinctively wonderful in a painting by Van Gogh, and to turn aside saying, 'After all, human beings are only particularly dexterous animals with opposable thumbs.' Fascinated as one may be by books about ethology, warmly as one may admire people who live among animals and get to know them as truly fellow creatures, it need not be intellectual snobbery to begin to feel that a desert island needs to be provided with some discs of Shakespeare and Mozart.

Human beings are distinctively different from computers on the one hand and animals on the other. Attempts to characterize their uniqueness fairly are not confined solely to traditional notions of rationality. Calculating and arguing are not always the greatest human achievements. For example, Anthony Kenny in the 1971–2 Gifford Lectures was happy to point out that Aristotle defined man 'not as a rational animal but as a choosing agent'.[7] This positive emphasis on choice is still only a start. Kenny went on at once to suggest that Aristotle's definition still leaves out 'the element of creativity.' Here he found 'the characteristic which, if any does, separates us both from inert artifacts and from brute beasts.' It is worth seizing upon Kenny's 'if any does' and giving it some emphasis.

The particular excellences of humanity can be appreciated all the better if creativity is not treated as one distinct gift, present in people but not in other creatures, or present in a few people and absent elsewhere. Inspiration is multifarious and its range and variety are practically unlimited. There is no need for it to be evenly spread. Most of us have no outstanding genius and are no less fully human for that. We belong to the species which has produced Socrates, Michelangelo and Einstein and their achievements belong to us too. Their work was done, so to say, on our behalf. Unshared, it would be pointless. In a better world, where the lamb might lie down with the lion, one might be able to think likewise of human creativity as available in some way on behalf of all our fellow creatures.

---

[7] Kenny *et al.*, *The Nature of Mind*, 1972, p. 11

Can one think at all about human creativity in the better world to come which our tradition foretells? Anything we try to say about another life than this cannot be said in plain prose. The most we know is hints and hopes, and what we believe we cannot describe. Yet ideas which can be expressed only in poetry can still be true or false. If they are true, it is because there is some reality of which they give a true picture.

So we have to ask whether it could possibly give a true picture to give importance, beyond this life, to the human creativity we value so much in this. Christian people believe firmly that this life is not all; but if they try to be too specific about heavenly hopes, piety reminds them that human excellence is due to be 'lost in wonder, love and praise.'[8] It certainly looks as if the ones who are building on a rock must be those who simply hope for the vision of God, without trying to say anything more about life in heaven.

Yet before coming to a stop here there is more to be said, in line with the New Testament accounts of the teaching of Christ. The Gospels constantly portray the kingdom of God as celebrating, feasting and making merry together. Behind these down-to-earth word pictures there is the convincing assumption of the lasting importance of individual human existence in the eyes of the Creator, summed up in the saying that the God of Abraham, Isaac and Jacob is not the God of the dead but of the living.

Abraham is a different person from Isaac, and Isaac from Jacob. Their fulfilment is not likely to be monochrome. When people 'glorify God and enjoy him for ever', the offerings they hope to bring will surely not be undifferentiated. If the 'divine service' of eternity means more than a 'lip-service' of perpetual hymn-singing, it needs, so to say, some variegated filling:

> Let every creature rise and bring
> Peculiar honours to our king.[9]

The diverse vocations of the individual creatures alive on earth need not turn out to be trivial in God's eyes nor insignificant in the kingdom of heaven. Sophisticated believers can responsibly allow themselves to join with unsophisticated believers in affirming that there has been some point in evolution and that the multiplicity of creaturely ways of life are meant to be fulfilled not repudiated.

---

[8] Charles Wesley, 'Love divine, all love excelling', *Hymns Ancient & Modern*, No. 520
[9] Isaac Watts, 'Jesus shall reign where'er the sun', *Hymns Ancient & Modern*, No. 220; see Oppenheimer, 1988, pp. 131–2 and 2001, pp. 121–4

Chapter 15

Owing

Two things fill the mind with ever increasing wonder and awe, the more often and the more intensely reflection is occupied with them: the starry heaven above me and the moral law within me.

Kant, 1788, Conclusion

High among the excellent gifts of human creatures is the capacity to recognize these gifts. Christians of humanist inclination can be comfortable with the ancient myth of creation, that God called everything into existence and pronounced it all good. They will be puzzled, to the point of feeling rebellious, by the development of the story, that what went wrong and destroyed human innocence was eating the fruit of the tree of knowledge. Surely knowledge is good, and the knowledge of good and evil is an aspect of human glory not of human sinfulness?

It is tempting to say, So much the worse for Genesis, if it teaches us to be afraid of moral understanding. It is natural and it feels pious to believe that our knowledge of values, far from being deplorable, is even part of the meaning of being made in God's image. We may want to go so far as to locate our superiority to 'brute beasts' here. Animals indeed are innocent, but they cannot be called virtuous. Moral good and evil are not part of their experience. They do not have values. They cannot be counted as moral beings: we can. So was the Fall of humankind really no fall but a step up? We cannot help using our moral capacity as a basis to build on.

It does not appear that animals have moral capacity. Individual apes can be better or worse parents; horses can be hard-working or lazy, placid or bad-tempered. Maybe they can be trained or taught. They may respond to kindness or to discipline. What does not make sense is to ascribe credit or blame to them for doing well or ill. It is still less sensible to blame animals whose natural ways of doing well are not to our liking. Hungry lions are not cruel and cuckoos who trespass in other birds' nests are not selfish. Midges are maddening but they do not set out to annoy.

By contrast, dogs have entered into a special relationship with humankind. They have left their wolf ancestry behind and become members of the human community.[1] Puppies can be educated, like children, into a way of life which includes something like the authority of conscience. A dog who has committed the social gaffe of barking at someone he should have recognized seems clearly embarrassed. A puppy who is found to have chewed a shoe behaves like a sinner who has been caught out. Though it is overdoing it to say that he repents of his transgression, he surely feels something akin to remorse. That is why people suggest that a dog's master who has taught him how to behave is almost literally his God. The faithfulness of a dog is a kind of piety.

We generally do not include wild animals nor even most domesticated animals in our moral community. Cats live in people's houses and cows live in people's fields and their owners love and cherish them, but do not ascribe to them the same moral status as people. Some would call that 'speciesist'. The concept of a moral being needs more sorting out. If we understand a 'moral being' as a moral agent, someone who has duties and deserves praise or blame, then it is possible to think of dogs as, so to say, honorary moral beings, in contrast with giraffes in the bush who are not moral beings, and also, it must be said, in contrast with babies in arms are not moral beings yet.

Having obligations, being capable of doing right or wrong, is one acceptable way of defining what counts as a moral being, but this is not the only way. Perhaps a creature should be included in the human moral world, without qualifying as a moral agent, by being what has been called a 'moral patient'.[2] Though giraffes do not have duties and babies are too young to have duties, it makes sense to say that duties may be owed *to them* and moral claims made on their behalf. Humane people may well ask Bentham's question, whether they can suffer, and on that basis include all sentient animals as fellow creatures. They have a sort of place in our moral community and ought to have at least some ethical consideration for their own sakes. It would follow that it is a moral wrong to starve a cat, to experiment blithely on a chimpanzee, or to leave an injured rabbit dying in pain.

---

[1]   See Sharpe, 2005; Lorenz, *Man Meets Dog*, 1954; Brooks, 1987–8.
[2]   Regan, 2004, pp. 151–6

A robin redbreast in a cage
Puts all heaven in a rage[3]

and pulling the wings off a butterfly is callous. It may well be wrong to keep hens in batteries or calves in crates, or to be unconcerned about conditions in abattoirs. 'How much does this creature mind?' is always a fair question.

Animals do not need 'knowledge of good and evil', or the capacity to discover values, for values to apply to them and for human beings to owe objective duties to them. The moral significance of this or that creature does not depend directly upon whether it is capable of understanding the world we are all living in, still less of analyzing it. Intelligence may go with greater or less vulnerability to fear, discomfort or pain. Animal suffering must be recognized as a matter of significance by anyone who repudiates relativism and who understands that morality is independent of what we choose to think.

Once people acknowledge a real moral order which they have not invented, the traditional and tempting distinction between people and animals, that animals lack moral autonomy, has to fall. Of course animals do not decide for themselves what is good or bad nor devise their own values; but then only relativists suppose that is what human beings should do. For people who are not relativists, real good and evil are not invented, but have to be discovered, or missed, in the intractable complexities of every situation. People and animals can inhabit one moral world where what happens is objectively better or worse, whether or not any particular individual is capable of comprehending what living in a moral world means.

Human beings do claim to be capable of comprehending what living in a moral world means. Therefore they cannot deny that all is far from well and that a great deal of what happens really is worse, not better. Often it is worse because of human actions. The myth of the Fall remains an only too convincing way of describing the human condition. We may be allowed not to swallow it whole. If we may put respectfully aside, as something we cannot readily fit in to our tradition, the strange notion that becoming a moral being is itself the first sin, the convincing message will stand out the more clearly. As soon as human creatures do become moral beings, as soon as they have the option of wrongdoing, they do wrong. Our innocence was lost before it was ever put into practice. We are fallen creatures from the start. So far, so bad.

---

[3]   William Blake, 'Auguries of innocence'

The both/and of glory and wretchedness which seems to place us above the other animals also places us beneath them. As creative and rational creatures, people are glorious. As fallen creatures, they are sinners and have been sinners all along. As usual, these two contrary statements must somehow be set side by side, not cancelling each other out. The truth of the one does not refute, nor even diminish, the truth of the other. Doing justice to what human beings are must somehow comprehend both their real glory and their real disgrace.

On the one hand, 'The heart of man is deceitful above all things and desperately wicked'[4] cannot be reduced to 'We haven't done very well'. On the other hand, our theology announces the goodness, not the depravity, of creatures as primary. 'God saw everything that he had made and behold, it was very good' is not to be reduced to 'fairly good'. Then human sin appears as a frightful complication, not as a contradiction, of the value of creation. It is the grandest good that lets in the greatest harm. The insight that 'the worst is the corruption of the best' indicates that evil is in its nature parasitic upon good. Badness is not a free-standing alternative, like a candidate in a democratic election, offering a viable alternative to goodness. Christians have not thought of the devil as a rival God but as a fallen angel.

To be in a position to appreciate the created excellence of human beings, one needs to say a great deal more about what makes human life in itself positively worth living. There is more to human existence than our position in distinction from other creatures. Comparing and contrasting variegated human capacities and ways of life with the variegated capacities and ways if life of other creatures is enlightening and constructive as far as it goes. To stop here, looking over human shoulders to keep identifying likenesses and differences between ourselves and other animals, would unduly limit the scope and splendour of what goodness, truth and beauty mean for humanity. The relative ethical status of human and non-human animals is not the only question which matters morally.

To be capable of seeing what values mean is to be capable of reflecting on glory, integrity, kindness, generosity, heroism, genius, beauty, wonder. Human beings may be the only creatures to whose ways of living most of these categories can be directly and unequivocally applied. To accept the idea that we are special is not insensitive nor shocking, provided that we attend to the characteristic gifts of our own species in appreciative humility not arrogance. It is entirely

[4] *Jeremiah* 17.9

in order for human beings to be most concerned about human beings, what they can do, what they should do, what matters to them: just as it is in order for people to mind about their own families and love them best.

One thing people, unlike animals, are often obliged to do is repent of their transgressions. Thinking of animals as sinners is on the edge of fantasy. When beloved and loving domestic pets are badly behaved they are supposed to mend their ways, but not to ask for forgiveness. Penitence is, so to say, a human speciality. No account of human nature, whether pessimistic or optimistic, can leave out the fact that they have left undone those things which they ought to have done and done those things which they ought not to have done.[5]

The repentance which is a compulsory feature of human living is another example of the paradoxical relationship between the best and the worst. Not only is the worst evil apt to be the corruption of the best good. The converse is also true, that the best good may, in the end, turn out to be a harvest growing out of the worst harm. Victory is even better than success without effort.[6] Edwin Muir wrote movingly of the 'blossoms of grief and charity' which need to be watered from the cloudy skies of earth.[7]

'*O felix culpa*' announces the Roman missal. 'O happy fault, which has earned such a mighty Redeemer'. The human capacity to sin and be sorry opens up positive possibilities of human glory. 'There will be more joy in heaven over one sinner who repents than over ninety-nine righteous persons who need no repentance'.[8] Faulty men and women may find that they can give even more delight to their Maker than troops of innocent animals who have never strayed from their natural created goodness.

It is time to pick up again the problem of evil, which can never be left out of account for long. According to the Christian Gospel, the Creator is able to meet the sins of human creatures with astonishing forgiveness, by paying the price of reconciliation. There are many theories of what it can mean to say that God-made-man *atoned* for the sins of the whole world. Some of these explanations can make the merciful God look heartless, legalistic or masochistic. If one is going to say something like, 'He endured, instead of us, the punishment

[5] The General Confession from Morning Prayer in the *Book of Common Prayer*
[6] See Oppenheimer, 2001, p. 115
[7] Edwin Muir, 'One foot in Eden', *Collected Poems 1921–1958*; quoted by permission of Faber & Faber.
[8] *Luke* 15.7

we deserved', one ought not to seem to imply that what most people have deserved is crucifixion. Indeed, has anyone merited such a horrible penalty? A God who made fallible creatures, put them in such a troubled world as this, and then looked down from on high and told them that it was their own fault and that torture would be a fair punishment, would not be a just God.

To keep a firm hold of the doctrine of creation offers more hope of understanding. Because creating and being created is a two-way relationship in which creatures owe their existence to their Maker, one can dare to say that the decision to create gives rise to responsibilities. A God who can be worshipped may be compared to an artist, who is carrying out an immense work and values it enough to be accountable for it and bear its cost. The cost of creation includes all the pains of the world which conscious creatures have to bear. The death of Christ can be interpreted as God's direct, as it were 'hands-on', experience of what it means to be a victim, to suffer and be hurt. That could suggest how it makes sense to say that Christ had to die to earn our deliverance.

The terms of reference for the doctrine of atonement are broader than human sins and include the groaning and travailing of the whole creation. Humane people are bound to bear in mind the horror of a tsunami or the sufferings of sick children. Animal lovers are not likely to forget the natural pains of innocent animals as a particularly intractable aspect of the problem of evil.

It is facile to suppose that if only all the blame could be allocated to the primal sin of humankind, and then forgiven, the problem would be solved. Dinosaurs suffered long before people sinned. As usual, it is more promising to take a longer way round. Christians who want to understand must recognize the problem of a whole good creation corrupted. They may keep on taking to heart the affirmation that the Creator was willing to bear the cost of making good. Then they may be able to consider what, if anything, can ever make tragedy redeemable; and to allow faith to be look hopefully for old or new signs that the worthwhileness of life will become apparent at last.[9]

---

[9] See Oppenheimer, 2001, e.g. p. 121

Chapter 16
Forgiving

Isabella: Why, all the souls that were were forfeit once;
And He that might the vantage best have took
Found out the remedy.

Measure for Measure, II. 2. 73

Honest confidence in atonement, the faith that God and creatures are reconciled, must be based upon sensitivity to the evils which need atonement, including the undeserved earthquakes and cancers and the hardships which seem to be nobody's fault. Faith depends on the premise that the Creator of everything there is takes ultimate responsibility for what the world is like.

Believers may not proceed to shift the whole blame on to their Maker. Minding about the troubles which beset all mortal creatures is no substitute for sombre acknowledgment that human beings are sinful. The whole problem of evil includes all the particular misdeeds of fallen humanity. The Atonement is not only for generalized evil but for specific wrongdoing, of which the crucifixion of Christ was an extreme example. All human beings are part of the interrelated world in which Emmanuel, 'God with us' was put to death.

The traditional understanding of the meaning of atonement has been that God, and only God, is 'good enough to pay the price of sin'.[1] On that basis, mercy belongs to God alone. It would be presumptuous, even blasphemous, to make light of the conviction that every sin is first of all an offence against God. And yet: it is our fellow creatures who are evidently harmed by most of the sins which people commit. The question recurs: How, after all, can it be God who has the sole right to be merciful and pardon, from heaven, all the unforgiven injuries people do to one another? How can anything but being hurt by one's own enemies give anyone the right to absolve sinners?

The needful moral answer to the problem of sins has to be the same as the needful moral answer to the problem of evil, that the

---

[1]   Mrs C.F. Alexander, 'There is a green hill far away', *Hymns A & M*, No. 332

merciful Creator 'up there' is not remote from suffering. The doctrine of the atonement is that God came to earth, suffered from
human cruelty and injustice and experienced at first hand the actual
wrongs which need to be forgiven.

Discussions of forgiveness, human or divine, are apt to turn into
sermons.[2] The risk must be run and the argument pursued, if one
means to affirm that people's wretchedness and people's excellence
are part of one story, because there are perplexing questions about
the ethics of mercy. Christians in particular need to sort out their preconceptions about what forgiving does and does not mean.

Much is made of the conviction that God's forgiveness is 'unconditional'; but that is an over-simplification. It is God's *love* which
should be described as unconditional. This is the kind of unlimited
indestructible love expected of parents, which is part of the meaning
of calling God 'Father'. Unconditional *forgiveness*, which makes no
demands whatever, is more like condoning sin than putting it right.
In the New Testament, forgiveness is not actually unconditional.
God's people have been clearly told that something is required of
them.

The clear condition upon which the mercy of God is offered is not
virtue, nor making amends, nor even penitence, but mercy to one
another.[3] Unless people forgive, their own sins cannot be forgiven.
This priority was set up before the Lord died or rose again, before
there was a doctrine of atonement and a church to try to understand
it. People who say the Lord's Prayer expressly accept as a condition
for being forgiven by God that they are forgiving the people who
have sinned against them.

It is a pleasingly paradoxical idea that the godlike difference
between human beings and other animals might be the capacity to
forgive sins, rather than any achieved human excellence. If mercy
belongs to the 'image and likeness of God', maybe the creatures who
can enter into this are the ones who find out what mercy means
because they themselves need it. Animals, one may suppose, belong
unselfconsciously in the Kingdom already[4] without learning what it
means to receive mercy or to give it. They are not to be expected to be
sorry for doing wrong, or to forgive the wrongs people commit
against them. in the way that people have to be sorry and forgive.

---

[2] This chapter is indeed based upon a Cambridge University Sermon on
'Grievances', preached May 1, 1983, and printed in *Theology*, January 1988.
[3] e.g. *Matthew* 18.32
[4] e.g. *Psalm* 104

The attractive notion of 'man' as the merciful animal can still not be taken for granted. On the one hand, the contrast with fellow creatures is not sharp. Ill-treated beasts of burden are characteristically submissive rather than vengeful. Animals kill for food and kill in self-defence; but they do not go to war. Konrad Lorenz pointed out that though doves, the symbols of peace, may peck each other to death, a ferocious wolf has mercy on a defeated foe.[5]

On the other hand, 'the way that people have to forgive one another' is not a plain and straightforward notion. The magnificent psalmist who took the wings of the morning even claimed credit for not overlooking wrongs and for making God's foes his own: 'Do not I hate them, O Lord, that hate thee ... ? Yea, I hate them right sore: even as though they were mine enemies.'[6] For him, condoning evil was a more serious fault than cherishing grudges. He bore witness that he had not neglected to put God's enemies in the category of the 'hateable'.

Since his day, things have changed. God has made a new covenant with his chosen people. They are commanded now to get rid of this category of the 'hateable', to get rid of it altogether, not just to reorganize it. So Christians have to turn their backs upon the straightforward partisanship of the psalmist. An enemy is there to be forgiven, to be blessed and prayed for. In a way, he is the most promising kind of neighbour, the test and guarantee of one's unselfishness.

Thomas Traherne expounded Christian duty with persuasive vigour:

> Yet you must Arm yourself with Expectations of their Infirmities, and resolv nobly to forgive them: not in a sordid and Cowardly maner, by taking no notice of them: nor in a Dim and Lazy maner, by letting them alone: but in a Divine and Illustrious maner by chiding them meekly, and vigorously rendering and showering down all kinds of Benefits.[7]

That would make an encouraging peroration to a practical discourse on forgiveness. Of course that is what it must be like to forgive, and people can do it if they try: or can they? If mercy is such a basic human attribute it needs to be better understood. What we have so far is a hopeful way of asking out a question, not an answer: a destination not a route, still less a short cut. Some of us are troubled by both the practice and the theory of forgiveness.

[5]   Lorenz, 1966
[6]   *Psalm* 139.21
[7]   Traherne, *Centuries* I, 1958, 84

What is it to forgive and how are human beings to set about doing it? Several inadequate accounts can be readily rejected. Forgiveness is different from letting someone off from a punishment. We sometimes believe that punishment is still necessary, and often it is irrelevant. Forgiveness is more than *saying* 'I forgive you': to say anything may not be the point at all. It is more than abstaining from revenge: yet what is this 'more'? The manufacture of forgiving feelings cannot be necessary. Forgiveness is supposed not to depend upon conditions: but what is this transaction which requires neither party to do anything in particular? If people find it hard to say what forgiveness is, perhaps they can try to show it in their lives? Here the shoe pinches more tightly than ever.

Christian would be sensible to repudiate the insidious conviction that they are meant to be doormats. Pious people meekly, indeed weakly, accept oppression, and set about forgiving their enemies not in Traherne's 'Divine and Illustrious maner' but sometimes with a spinelessness that destroys sympathy, and sometimes with a smugness that seems to endow 'the meek shall inherit the earth' with an ironical and intolerable meaning far from beatitude. Turning the other cheek is distorted into yet another recipe for salvation, uncreative in human terms and perhaps not even benevolent. Shaw held this paradoxical kind of legalism up to mockery in his portrayal of the converted fighter Ferrovius in *Androcles and the Lion*.

It is bad enough to see people miserably failing to stand up for *themselves*. It is worse to see them almost corruptly condoning harms that have been done to other people, and all in the name of religion. One warms to Gibbon's account of King Clovis, who on being instructed in the Passion story exclaimed 'with indiscreet fury, "Had I been present at the head of my valiant Franks, I would have revenged his injuries"'.[8] One does not warm to people who make light of other people's wrongs, even in the name of the Gospel: compassionate anger is more human and more moral, and it is grievous not to be able to call it more Christian.

But might forgiveness be one of those things hidden from the wise and understanding and revealed to babes? Real forgiveness, human or divine, seems unsuitable for cool dissection. People who are standing back far enough from the hurt that needs forgiving are standing back too far to see. Ought they not simply to be asking God for his help?

---

[8]   *The History of the Decline and Fall of the Roman Empire*, ch. XXXVIII

The case is not so straightforward. In the prayer Christians have been taught to make, they do not *ask* their heavenly Father to help them to do this difficult feat of forgiving: they say they are doing it already. They let it be made a condition for God's mercy upon them. So if they are confused and doubtful about what it is they are supposed to be doing, their situation is an awkward one. It is no good saying sadly like a character in a poem by Browning,

> I would we were boys as of old
> In the field, by the fold:
> His outrage, God's patience, man's scorn
> Were so easily borne![9]

The intellectual difficulty is that forgiveness is 'either unjustified or pointless'.[10] Aurel Kolnai set the problem, that when the sinner is not sorry, forgiveness is only condonation. If the sinner is truly sorry, there is nothing now to forgive. The more promising answer which Kolnai offered (p. 97) is that what forgiveness does is anticipate repentance. It goes to meet a change of heart in the offender, gambling generously upon his restoration. So, as exemplifying 'an attitude of *trust* in the world' (p. 105) forgiveness can be ethically defended, when it happens. But there remains the practical difficulty, how human beings can set about achieving it.

Of course Christians do not find themselves without help in this most central problem. It would be incredible if in two thousand years wise and holy believers had not by example and precept demonstrated to one another the workings of mercy. But when wisdom and holiness tidy away the problem with a sort of warm enfolding blanket which only covers up awkward crumples underneath, then something more needs to be said.

Of course the complete answer must be to hate the sin and love the sinner. But 'hating the sin' in practice is apt to mean anything from the relentless ferocity of the persecutor to the vague regret of the worldly colleague. Neither of these is forgiveness. And when one turns to 'loving the sinner', it is easy to slip into knee-jerk tolerance, that dreary automatic justifying of other people which is nearly as unconstructive as obsessive self-justification. 'Of course he didn't mean any harm. It was all my fault.' John Donne in his poetical litany asked to be delivered from

[9]   *Dramatic Lyrics*, 'After'
[10] Kolnai, 'The logical paradoxy of forgiveness', p. 99

… indiscreet humility
Which might be scandalous
And cast reproach on Christianity.

It might indeed.

At this stage people begin to talk about forgiveness as restoring right relationships; and such understanding is, literally, heavenly. The questions which must still be asked are about the fragments that have to be left over because there is nothing there to restore: the damage done by the unknown criminal, the casual but bitter offence caused by someone who does not in the least want one's friendship, the insensitivity of the bureaucrat, the animosity of the political opponent, the unreliability of the charmer who must not be trusted any more, the patronizing smugness of the prig who is not human enough to be in the wrong: and all these still more bafflingly when it is other people who are being made to suffer. It is impertinent, both in the old sense of 'irrelevant' and in the newer sense of 'presumptuous', to imagine oneself establishing happy relationships where the truth is so intractable. So Donna Elvira might dream of forgiving Don Giovanni.

No doubt what is needed is to 'will people's good' and a saint can give this real substance. For average believers it may seem like an empty formula, or worse, a tacit invitation to play God. If this one repented and that one relented, how we would welcome them back into the fold!

All this argument is skirting round the most fundamental answer, that what forgiveness does with evil is quench it, meet it with peaceful endurance so that the poison spreads no further. 'The buck stops here' is a rough but fair summary of an essential part of the theology of atonement. The miserable cycle of hurt and hate can be stopped, and Christians of all people ought to be able to partake in its stopping. It would be defeatist to deny that they can and do, from St Stephen praying, 'Lord, lay not this sin to their charge', to prisoners of conscience today who refuse to let bitterness overcome them.

Of course that kind of forgiveness is the true solution, but the worst is the corruption of the best. What is more real in most people's experience than the inspiring patience of a saint is the disheartening damage that ensues when rage pent up in the name of forbearance bursts out in the end, the unkind half-meant things that say themselves; and, no better, the sour or sickly diminishment of people who cannot be angry. Sitting on safety valves is not a valuable sort of religious exercise. It is tempting to believe in despondency that 'Only God can forgive sins.'

If the serenity of real sanctity has to be achieved already as a condition for even asking for forgiveness, one's state is parlous. Each of these valid answers to the theoretical and practical difficulties about the meaning of forgiveness — hate the sin but not the sinner, restore relationships, quench the evil — leaves a residue of human inadequacy. Each of them is deeply true, at a stage which has not yet been attained.

To solve the problems would be to have reached the next stage; but at least one can take a nearer look at them. If the heights of holiness are out of reach, a worthwhile expedition in the foothills might take the form of a small-scale but serious attempt at honesty.

First then, can one make any approach to hating the sin and loving the sinner? One can stop trying to find plausible meanings for the love of enemies, when really one finds them simply detestable. It is more practical to focus one's mind on the intellectual conviction that strange as it may seem God loves the sinner. One can be simply anthropomorphic and consider that a breach between brothers and sisters is a hurt to their parent, whatever the rights and wrongs of the question. To look upon a hostile human being as a child of God is neither to try to play God oneself nor merely to suppress one's indignation. It could be the beginning of a way to dislodge implacable resentment. Whatever forgiveness is, it must be easier to do it for someone else's sake than on principle.

Secondly, it is true that sometimes relationships *can* be built or rebuilt after offence. To see what this might mean, one can try putting oneself at the receiving rather than the giving end, so as to get a sight of the notion of forgiveness on its home ground.

What does a human being need who needs to be forgiven? At least that question comes before the problem of how to be grand and good enough to forgive other people. Surely the answer is, indeed, St Paul's basic notion of *justification by faith*. People ask in various ways for mercy, meaning all sorts of things like another chance, or a formal pardon, or help with the mess they have made, or a reconciliation. But whatever people ask for, or are too proud or timid to ask for, what they generally crave for is justification, being in the right. If 'being in the right' sounds Pharisaical, as it does, one can use Catholic or Protestant jargon and talk about 'being in a state of grace' or being 'right with' God and one another. The point about forgiveness is that this human craving is not hopeless. The truth that some people know instinctively and that the Protestant reformers rediscovered as a revelation worth living and dying for, is that justification *is* available but is not to be earned.

What human beings need, whether from God or from one another, is not to have to justify themselves by their works. They need to be set up and treated as if they mattered. They need to be given attention as people, without their failings being treated as characteristic or their good behaviour bargained over. If they are treated so, they will need less forgiving. In other words, they need grace. It is a pity to shrink the idea of grace into a technicality. It is, as it were, the light one person sheds on another. If God's grace is sunlight, human grace is the real though derived light of the moon; but the ghostly coolness of moonlight is no adequate analogy for the sustaining reality of an uncensorious, but not unexacting, personal regard. So forgiveness, divine or human, is the way grace, divine or human, is projected upon badness. Forgiveness is no peculiar activity in which human beings usurp the prerogative of God but a way for them to project the grace of God. To understand what it costs would be to understand atonement.

To justify the *un*godly is the prerogative of God, when human grace has reached the end of its tether. What is to happen when forgiveness is, humanly speaking, out of the question? Where is 'justification' to get a purchase where honesty finds only deep misery or bitterness or the sort of abiding coldness where grace is in eclipse? The third answer, the one most needed, to the question of what forgiveness means, that unconquerable love can somehow *quench* the evil, is the answer that seems least possible. If this quenching is something that only God can do, where does human forgiving come in and what good is it?

One must be realistic enough to acknowledge the objective existence of wrongs. In dealing with evil, forgiveness is facing something real.

> Abel's blood for vengeance
> Pleaded to the skies.[11]

Since blood has no vocal chords, it is easy to think of this as a metaphor through and through, especially when one is trying to disapprove of what the metaphor means. One might instead go along with the metaphor: there really are states of affairs which 'cry out' for justice. Grievances are at least as real as sins. Downtrodden Israelites

---

[11] Edward Caswall, 'Glory be to Jesus', *Hymns Ancient & Modern*, No. 107

knew that they had a case against their enemies in the heavenly court. The righteous man begged God for judgement, not in fear but in hope. Confidence that God will pardon sin is presumption if it means that God will ignore. When it is other people's wrongs that are in question, it is heartless to suppose that nowadays God takes no heed of them.

Something has to be done with grievances, and pretending that they do not exist is not doing something with them. The New Testament is not about overlooking grievances but about the cost of dealing with them. A simple penal theory of the Atonement says too crudely that sinners must be punished and that God in Christ took their punishment. There are more sensitive ways of explaining the faith that God is not less than a just judge, but more. If in God's creative mercy all things are eventually to be brought to good, the fact that some of God's children are bitterly aggrieved is, so to say, part of God's problem. Simply to pardon offenders over the heads of the people they have hurt is to condone. Somehow God has to 'make atonement'.

If our grievances are real, they are our very own, and nobody has the right to confiscate them if we want to cherish them. It is a real question what to do with them. If there are human rights at all, people have a plain right to withhold forgiveness. Here is a decision which animals are surely not in a position to make. One reason why it is apt to be denied that animals can have rights, although animals can surely be wronged, is that the concept of animals claiming their rights does not make evident sense. Even less does it make sense to think of animals forgoing their rights.

Being made in God's image involves partaking in God's problem of what to do about offences. People who are disposed to try to forgive may make the positive decision not to claim their rights. They cannot suppress their grievances, but they may hope to be able to *sacrifice* them. A sacrifice is not merely abolished: it is offered up. To forgive could be to forgo the enjoyment of a real grievance by making an offering of it. Human beings can set about positively entrusting their wrongs to God.

Old Testament believers could assure themselves that God would at last vindicate them. Under the new covenant it is plain that God will do nothing so simple, that somehow or other the ungodly are to be not damned but justified. Forgiving is giving God a free hand. It is not presumptuous to see oneself and one's own injuries as part of the problem of creation. If St Paul could hope to fill up what was lacking in the sufferings of Christ,[12] in due modesty his fellow Christians can take the chance not to add to the cost of atonement.

People may feel as if they are living in a cold and wintry world, surrounded by wrongs like drifts of snow. Snow makes a good analogy for grievance, including the fact that it is fun to play with. Lovingly shaped into a snowman with eyes and nose and mouth, it hangs about indefinitely in unsightly lumps. Newly-fallen snow is insubstantial stuff, melting as it lands when the ground is warm, hardly part of the real material world at all. But when it has settled and has been trodden down, it is solid and dangerous and can break our bones. We sweep it and grit it and mind our step until one day the sun comes out. The warmth of spring dissolving the impacted mounds and ridges is a tangible image of grace. It is to be hoped that there are no perpetual snows.

---

[12] *Colossians* 1.24

Chapter 17

Praising

Now unto God the Father, God the Son and God the Holy Spirit
be ascribed, as is his most just due, all might, majesty, dominion,
power and glory, now and for ever.[1]

Human beings do what they ought to know is wrong. They need to be
forgiven by God and one another; and in this they are different from
the other animals. To go so far as to single out this need and possibility
as *the* basic distinctiveness of human beings would be ungratefully
self-deprecating. There is more that is special about people than their
misdeeds. In the biblical story of creation, sin comes unhappily early,
but not quite at the very beginning. The primary announcement that
'God saw that it was good' is pronounced first over every kind of
creature. Then the positive and particular excellence of human beings
is announced, that they are formed in the image of God. They have
some special kind of similarity to their Creator.

But the ancient myth is thoroughly realistic, that from the start
they begin to go wrong. Humanity is banished from Paradise. Must
it be concluded that human excellence is wholly lost? Total depravity is too dire. The terms of reference for human life are not simple,
but still require the paradoxical combination of unworthiness and
glory. Badness does not cancel created goodness; nor do badness
and goodness dilute each other and leave people merely quite good.

What makes it possible to keep hold of the paradox without
despair or presumption is God's forgiveness. Mercy, said Portia, 'is
an attribute to God himself'.[2] Loving-kindness belongs fundamentally to the character of God the Creator. The Lord our God is 'gra-
cious and merciful, slow to anger and of great kindness'.[3] This
teaching is thoroughly familiar to generations of users of the *Book of*

[1]   Ascription traditionally used after Church of England sermons at Morning
      or Evening Prayer. I am particularly grateful to Dr E.A. Livingstone for the
      trouble she took over looking into the origins of this tradition for me.
[2]   *The Merchant of Venice*, IV. 1. 192
[3]   *Joel* 2.13, used at the beginning of Morning Prayer, *Book of Common Prayer*

Common Prayer. God's clemency is not to be counted as an extra benefit, an 'add-on', which is available if we need it because fortunately for humankind mercy and holiness are not incompatible. Mercy is part of what is meant by God's holiness.

But mercy is not the total of holiness, nor the whole meaning of God's love. Forgiveness of sin is not the only blessing which fallen human beings can hope to receive. Human creatures are still capable of being endowed with their own 'peculiar honours' in order to offer them back to their King.[4]

'The end of man is to glorify God and enjoy him for ever' is the encouraging affirmation of the Shorter Catechism. Nowadays one must be careful not to allow 'man' to exclude women. Then one can move on further, beyond humanity, into another both/and. Nobody who takes the recurring 'God saw that it was good' in the first chapter of the Book of Genesis as inspired need restrict to human beings alone the possibility of glorifying the Creator. The role of 'Man', George Herbert declared, is to be '… the world's high priest: he doth present the sacrifice for all'.[5] The whole creation can be imagined as joining in the work of demonstrating the grandeur of its Maker. People are not excluded because they are sinful; nor are animals because they are inarticulate; nor are plants nor even rocks because they are unaware.

What human beings can do, because they are articulate, is glorify God with speech. The most straightforward way of giving glory is *praising*. Just as people are able to praise one another with words like 'Well done'; so they can praise their Creator with words like 'Glory to God in the highest'. One might choose to make a sharp distinction here between self-conscious creatures, whose duty and privilege it is to offer praise to God, and all the rest of nature, which remains in silent ignorance of how it pleases its Creator. The distinction is not invalid, but inadequate. Though only speakers can offer literal praise, the words of the Benedicite, 'O all ye works of the Lord, bless ye the Lord: praise him and magnify him for ever', are an apt and admirable metaphor. God is glorified by the whole creation. 'In Reason's ear', said Joseph Addison, the sun, the moon and the stars 'all rejoice

> And utter forth a glorious voice,
> For ever singing as they shine,
> 'The hand that made us is divine'.[6]

---

[4] See above, p. 109
[5] Herbert, *Works*, 'The church', 'Providence'
[6] Joseph Addison, 'The spacious firmament on high', *Hymns Ancient & Modern*, No. 662

The natural creation can be metaphorically included with people in praising God; and people can be literally included with the natural creation in magnifying the Creator.

The firm boundary between self-conscious creatures and all the others can be blurred. Then, when humanity is properly rooted in the world of nature, it is time to move the other way and reinstate the contrast. Human beings are still distinctive, particularly, but not only, in the use of speech. Whether or not they use words to express their praise, people have the gift of being aware of glory and making a positive conscious response. That is, they are able to worship.

Glorifying, praising and worshipping overlap with one another, but the differences are worth noticing. What *glorifying* means can be approached by considering the prosaic idea of doing somebody credit. Children can be a credit to their parents and pupils to their teachers. Likewise a creature can glorify its maker, simply by publicly existing. Planets, plants and people glorify God the Creator. The soul of the Madonna 'doth glorify the Lord'. A painted Madonna glorifies Raphael and the Lord is glorified by Raphael's handiwork.

Glory that is experienced and acknowledged in words becomes *praise*, praise of other people for all manner of excellences and praise to God for absolute holiness. It is proper to glorify and praise whatever can be discerned as wonderful, whether familiar or strange, natural, human or divine. Admiration and gratitude are life-enhancing human capacities.

The stage beyond praising is *worshipping*, which is glorifying and praising what is holy. Worship is more than admiration and gratitude. It is reverent veneration, inwardly felt and outwardly offered. Angels are imagined, and portrayed in works of art, as worshipping. Human beings, 'lower than the angels', are invited to join in; and one thinks one knows what is expected. Worship is expressed by speech or in silence and may be recognized by reverent actions, kneeling or bowing one's head, taking off one's shoes, putting one's hands together or holding them out.

It is still not self-evident what worship really means. The adoration which human creatures owe their Creator must be something more than saying prayers and going through the motions of piety, and something more than believing, as a matter of fact, that God is kind. It is tempting to suppose that only saints can really understand what it is to worship, and they are too absorbed in doing it to stop and analyse what they are doing. It is more usual for would-be worshippers to be granted hints and hopes,[7] encouraging but delicate, bursting like bubbles if one tries to handle them.

People who try to give some account of what worship is are apt to put the strongest emphasis upon God's almighty power. 'The fear of the Lord is the beginning of wisdom'.[8] That might seem to identify worship with an almost political surrender to overwhelming might. Such frightened self-abasement leads more directly into idolatry than into true religion. Terrifying power may coerce people into submission, but that kind of obedience is at best prudent and at worst ignoble. If capitulation is the best response to make, it hardly has much to do with what religious faith is supposed to be. Attempts to convey faith to others are bound to be unpersuasive. There is a more naïve approach to the meaning of worship which is more promising.

The idea which is missing from sheer power is the uncanny character of the supernatural, one might almost say its 'spookiness'. If sophisticated people are disdainful, they may be avoiding superstition at the cost of closing down a kind of sensitivity. The seemingly primitive notion of God's transcendent *awesomeness* captures the nature of holiness more adequately than notions about God's mighty force. Rudolph Otto's great book *The Idea of The Holy* gave a classic analysis of what it is that elicits worship. This experienced reality, for which he coined the word 'numinous', has two aspects. Holiness is the mystery which is *tremendum* and *fascinans*. The holy is tremendous, maybe terrifying, but not simply alarming. Otto's significant both/and is that this fearful mystery, far from being repellent, is essentially fascinating, attractive and wonderful.

If worship is valid at all, it is something which properly belongs to human nature. It is not something characteristic only of immaturity, still less something which happens to be left over from our animal ancestry. To set aside primitive religious awe as naïve would be as shallow as to set aside the creative inspiration of the Lascaut cave paintings as naïve. Both point forwards rather than backwards, at the start of something wonderful which characterizes the human spirit.

As usual, there is no need to be grudgingly possessive. Devout people need not try to refute Jane Goodall, the student of chimpanzees, who observed 'the ecstatic dance of chimps at the foot of a thundering waterfall and postulated a sense of awe and wonder'.[9] Human piety is not threatened if other creatures turn out to have some inkling of it.

---

[7] See Oppenheimer, 1973, pp. 52–4
[8] *Psalm* 111.10
[9] Barbour, *Nature, Human Nature and God*, 2002, p. 43

The difference between true worship and idolatry is not what the worshipper feels or does but for whom. Christians believe in the God of Abraham, Isaac and Jacob, not in Zeus or Amen Ra; nor, one hopes, in money, sex or the Führer. People who pray have become aware of a particular kind of claim whose authority they find supreme. They respond to it with an appropriate surrender which is humble but not base.

What Christian worship calls for is not only dutiful obedience but generous-mindedness, beginning to answer to the generosity of the God to whom it is offered. The analogy of falling in love is a good corrective to the legalism of obeying a ruler. A description which Austin Farrer applied to the human kind of worship which is marriage, 'the union of duty with delight',[10] could apply to the divine worship people try to offer to God.

Duty and delight are both characteristically expressed by bringing offerings. Primitive and mature, profound and naïve, are more tangled here than ever. Which is more childish, to suppose that human gifts will give *pleasure* to a God imagined as *like* us, or that they will succeed in *placating* a God whose ways are *not* our ways? 'Will the Lord be pleased with thousands of rams, with ten thousands of rivers of oil? Shall I give my first-born for my transgression, the fruit of my body for the sin of my soul?'[11]

When human beings have become too sophisticated to imagine that they can serve God by cooking God's dinner, or that they can give God a present they have brought as a happy surprise, or that they can buy off God's wrath with gifts, they come to realise that the only worthy offering is one's own self. This must be true, but it is not the last word.

First, one's own self is not really going to be a worthy offering. Only God's grace can overcome the mixed motives of human worship. Even when response really is sincere, only God's grace can expand its smallness enough to make it worthwhile. Second, what does giving one's self actually mean? How is anybody to set about making this offering? People cannot gift-wrap their selves or bind their selves upon the horns of an altar. How is 'self-offering' to be specific enough to mean anything?

Somebody's 'own self' is not an abstract idea of 'selfhood' but the particular individual that person is, with qualities more or less lovable which other people may not have. To offer oneself is to make

[10] Farrer, 'For a marriage', 1970, p. 137
[11] *Micah* 6.7

one's own life available, to put it at someone else's disposal. There are all manner of ways in which people put themselves at the disposal of their God, by reverently kneeling down in church, unselfconsciously doing works of mercy, or taking trouble to do their job as well as they can. Sincere worship is more variegated than devout people may be apt to imagine.

A besetting fault of sophisticated worship is vagueness. Another look at the ancient notion of offering a sacrifice can offer a corrective. To see the point of the time-honoured rites which go back into prehistory, one may think of them as a way of concentrating the service of God into the offering of some particular gift, some thing of one's own, which is dedicated to represent somebody's whole substance. The part is committed to stand in for the whole.[12]

That is the ideal, none the worse for being primitive. It is as corruptible as any other human ideal. The prophets of ancient Israel were by no means blind to the inadequacies of the temple rites as a way of worshipping God. With today's hindsight it is not hard to see that sacrifice may be legalistic and mercenary, or cruel and even grisly. Horror may be part of its appeal. The '*tremendum et fascinans*' of Otto's idea of the holy might make room for a kind of fascination one would not want to encourage. Have people sometimes half wanted to be heroic enough to offer their own children? Humane sceptics might find themselves cured of any lingering religious allegiance by the dread appeal of human sacrifice.

Believers learnt to offer the lives of animals instead of one another's lives. The paradoxical kind of dominion human beings are wont to claim over animals is poignantly in evidence, when the life of another creature is important enough to represent a human life but whatever 'selfhood' or sensitivity it may itself have are disregarded.

In Christian theology, the idea of sacrifice has gone a different way. According to Christian faith, the repetitive offering of victims in the Temple has given place to the one true sacrifice of Christ on the Cross.[13] People who are out of sympathy with the Christian Gospel, or impatient of theology, may assume that this represents a crude reversion to human sacrifice, especially when it is re-enacted in the Eucharist and the bread and wine are solemnly declared to stand for the body and blood of the Lord. If cannibalism were what sacredness meant, humanity would be better off without sacredness.

---

[12]   Quick, 1916, 'The principle of representative dedication'
[13]   *Hebrews* 10

The deep-seated ancient notion of sacrifice has more virtue in it than that. What is needed for renewed understanding is not to let go of materialistic notions of worship in favour of severely spiritual rites, but to take hold of a material thing and consecrate it to be a *sacrament*. The point is that human beings, who are physical creatures, discovered long ago that when everyday physical realities are dedicated as holy they can become 'means of grace.'

Often people put this belief into practice by saying a blessing over a meal and eating it together, entering into the basic human institution of hospitality. They keep *in touch* by offering one another food and drink, by which they convey all manner of meanings: goodwill, gratitude, comfort, happiness, reverence. People who dedicate their food-sharing to their God cherish the naïve but not misguided thought that the companionship of human beings is something that pleases their Maker.

The concept of people offering animals might be turned round. Because human beings are the creatures who can understand the idea of a sacrifice, they are the ones who ought to be able to represent all the other creatures. It might be said, in fanciful picture-language, that God made people for the very purpose of offering the praise of all creation for the glory of their Maker.[14] Human life may not generally look much like that, but it makes sense for believers to describe human life at its variegated best as conscious or unconsciously offered to God. The harshness of ancient sacrifice bears witness to the mysterious fact that an offering may cost a great deal because glory is not trivial.

A particular blessing of humanity is to find imagery to put what they believe into words. Nobody found better words than Thomas Traherne to express the notion that the Creator has purposes and can be pleased:

> This is very strange that God should Want. For in Him is the Fulnes of all Blessedness: He overfloweth Eternally ... It is Incredible, yet very Plain: Want is the Fountain of all his Fulness. Want in God is a Treasure to us. for had there been no Need He would not have Created the World, nor made us, nor manifested His Wisdom, nor Exercised His Power, nor beautified Eternity, nor prepared the Joys of Heaven. But He wanted Angels and Men, Images, Companions. And these He had from all Eternitie ... 'You must want like a GOD, that you may be satisfied like GOD. Were you not made in His Image?'[15]

[14]   See e.g. *Romans* 8. 19–23
[15]   Traherne, 1958, I, 41 and 44. See also above, p. 47

Bibliography

Books

Before 20th Century

Thomas Aquinas (1225–74), *Theological Texts*, ed. Thomas Gilby, *Summa Theologica*, 2a–2ae clxxxii 1, Oxford University Press, 1955.

Jeremy Bentham (1748–1832), *Introduction to the Principles of Morals and Legislation*, 1789.

Joseph Butler (1692–1752), *Fifteen Sermons Preached at the Rolls Chapel. Works*, Vol. II, ed. W.E. Gladstone, Clarendon Press 1896.

Lewis Carroll (1832–98), *Through the Looking-Glass*, 1871.

The Book of Common Prayer according to the use of the Church of England 1662.

Réné Descartes (1596–1650), *Discourse on Method*, 1637.

Edward Gibbon (1737–1794), *The History of the Decline and Fall of the Roman Empire*, 1776–1788.

David Hume (1711–1776), *Dialogues Concerning Natural Religion*, 1779.

Samuel Johnson (1709–84), Preface to *A Dictionary of the English Language*, 1755.

Immanuel Kant (1724–1804), *Critique of Practical Reason*, 1788.

Terence (c.190–158), *Heauton Timoroumenos*, 77.

Thomas Traherne (1636–1674), *Centuries of Meditations*, Oxford University Press, 1958.

George Herbert (1593–1633), *Works*, 'The church', 'Providence'

20th and 21st Centuries

J.L. Austin, *How to do Things with Words*, Clarendon Press, 1962.

A.J. Ayer, *Language, Truth and Logic*, Gollancz, First published 1936.

Paul and Linda Badham, *Immortality or Extinction?*, Macmillan, 1982.

John Austin Baker, *The Foolishness of God*, DLT, 1970.

I. Barbour, *Nature, Human Nature and God*, SPCK, 2002.

Karl Barth, *Ethics*, trans. Geoffrey W. Bromley, T & T Clark, 1981.

Melvyn Bragg, *The Adventure of English: The Biography of a Language*, Sceptre 2003.

S.R.L. Clark, *Animals and Their Moral Standing*, Cambridge University Press, 1997.

C. Deane-Drummond, *The Ethics of Nature*, Blackwell, 2004.

David DeGrazia, *Taking Animals Seriously: Mental Life and Moral Status*, Cambridge University Press, 1996.

Jared Diamond, *The Rise and Fall of the Third Chimpanzee*, Radius, 1991, Vintage, 1992.

C.H. Dodd, *The Fourth Gospel*, Cambridge University Press, 1953

Mircea Eliade, *A History of Religious Ideas*, University of Chicago, 1978.

Austin Farrer, *Love Almighty and Ills Unlimited*, Fontana, 1966.

Austin Farrer, *The End of Man*, SPCK, 1973.

Peter Gärdenfors, *How Homo Became Sapiens: On the Evolution of Thinking*, Oxford University Press, 2003.

Jane Goodall, *In the Shadow of Man*, revised ed., Phoenix paperback, 1988.

Ernest Gowers, *Plain Words*, Her Majesty's Stationery Office, 1954, revised edition by Bruce Fraser, 1973.

John Habgood, *The Concept of Nature*, DLT, 2002.

R.M. Hare, *The Language of Morals*, Clarendon Press, 1952.

Vicki Hearne, *Adam's Task*, Heinemann, 1986.

A.P. Herbert, *What a Word*, Methuen, 1935.

David Jenkins, *What is Man?*, SCM Press, 1970.

David Jenkins, *God, Jesus and Life in the Spirit*, SCM Press, 1988.

D.C. Johanson & M.A. Edey, *Lucy: The Beginnings of Humankind*, Granada, 1981.

Richard Johnstone-Scott, *Jambo: A Gorilla's Story*, Michael O'Mara, 1995

Helen Keller *The Story of My Life*, Doubleday, Page & Co, 1902.

A .J. P. Kenny, H.C. Longuet-Higgins, J. R. Lucas, C.C. Waddington, *The Nature of Mind*, Edinburgh University Press, 1972.

Wolfgang Köhler, *The Mentality of Apes* (1925), Pelican Books, 1957.

David Lambert, *The Cambridge Guide to Prehistoric Man*, CUP, 1987.

Richard Leakey & Roger Lewin, *Origins: The Emergence and Evolution of Our Species and its Possible Future*, Futura Macdonald & Co., 1977.

Richard Leakey, *The Making of Mankind*, Michael Joseph, 1981.

Richard Leakey, *Human Origins*, Hamish Hamilton, 1982.

C.S. Lewis, *The Four Loves*, Bles, 1960.

P. Liebermann, *Uniquely Human*, Harvard University Press, 1991.

Linden, *Apes, Men and Language*, Penguin, 1976.

Andrew Linzey, *Animal Rights*, SCM Press, 1976.

Andrew Linzey & Dan Cohn-Sherbok, *After Noah: Animals and the Liberation of Theology*, Mowbray, 1997.

Konrad Lorenz, *King Solomon's Ring*, Methuen, 1952.

Konrad Lorenz, *Man Meets Dog*, Methuen, 1954.

Konrad Lorenz, *On Aggression*, English edition, Methuen, 1966.

Arthur O. Lovejoy, *The Great Chain of Being*, OUP, 1953.

Mary Midgley, *Beast and Man: The Roots of Human Nature*, Harvester Press, 1979.

Mary Midgley, *Animals and Why They Matter*, Penguin, 1983.

Basil Mitchell, *The Justification of Religious Belief*, Macmillan, 1973.

Steven Mithen, *The Prehistory of the Mind*, Thames & Hudson, 1996.

Edwin Muir, *Collected Poems 1921–1958*, Faber & Faber, 1960.

Anders Nygren, *Agape and Eros*, trans. Philip S. Watson, reprinted Harper Torchbooks, 1969.

Rudolph Otto, *The Idea of the Holy*, trans. John W. Harvey, 2nd edition, 1950.

H.H. Price, *Thinking and Experience*, Hutchinson, 1953.

Oliver Quick,1916, Ch. IX. 2, 'The principle of representative dedication', *Essays in Orthodoxy*, Macmillan, 1916.

Tom Regan, *The Case for Animal Rights*, University of California Press, updated with a new preface, 2004.

Gilbert Ryle, *The Concept of Mind*, Hutchinson, 1949.

Lynne Sharpe, *Creatures Like Us?*, Imprint Academic, 2005.

Peter Singer, *Animal Liberation*, 1975; Pimlico (Random House) 1995 (2nd edn.)

P. Strawson, *Individuals: An Essay in Descriptive Metaphysics*, Methuen, 1959, pp.115–6.

Charlotte Uhlenbroek, *Talking with Animals*, Hodder & Stoughton, 2002.

Frans de Waal, *Good Natured: The Origins of Right and Wrong in Humans and Other Animals*, Harvard, 1996.

Ludwig Wittgenstein, *Tractatus Logico-Philosophicus*, 1918, 3rd impression, Kegan Paul, 1922.

Helen Oppenheimer, *Law and Love*, Faith Press, 1962.

— *Incarnation and Immanence*, Hodders, 1973.

— *The Character of Christian Morality*, 2nd edition revised and enlarged, Faith Press, 1974.

— The *Marriage Bond*, Faith Press, 1976.

— The *Hope of Happiness*, SCM Press, 1983.

— *Looking Before and After*, The Archbishop of Canterbury's Lent Book for 1988, Fount Paperbacks.

— *Marriage* (in series 'Ethics: our choices' ed. Stephen Platten), Mowbray, 1990.

— *Finding & Following*, SCM Press, 1994.

— *Making Good*, SCM Press, 2001.

— *Profitable Wonders* (anthology), SCM Press, 2003.

Collections

ed. Andrew Linzey and Dorothy Yamamoto, *Animals on the Agenda*, SCM Press, 1998.

ed. Peter Singer, *In Defense of Animals: The Second Wave*, Blackwell, 2006.

Reference Books

Encyclopaedia Britannica, 15th Edition, 1974 onward, Vol. 8, 'Hominidae', 'Homo erectus', 'Homo sapiens'.

Encyclopedia of Human Evolution and Prehistory, Garland, 1988, ed. I. Tattersall, E. Delson, and J. Van Couvering, 1988, 'Neanderthal behaviour'.

Oxford Encyclopedic English Dictionary, 1991.

Oxford Dictionary of Quotations, 5th edition, 1999.

The Oxford Dictionary of the Christian Church, ed. F.L. Cross, 3rd edition, 1997, ed. E.A. Livingstone.

Articles and Lectures

A M Allchin, 'The theology of nature in the eastern fathers and among Anglican theologians', in *Man and Nature*, ed. Hugh Montefiore, Collins, 1975.

John Benson, 'Duty and the beast', *Philosophy*, October, 1978.

D.H.M. Brooks, 'Dogs and slaves: genetics, exploitation and morality', *Proceedings of the Aristotelian Society*, 1987–8.

John Cottingham, Discussion: 'A brute to the brutes? Descartes' treatment of animals', *Philosophy*, October 1978.

Philip E. Devine, 'The moral basis of vegetarianism', *Philosophy*, October, 1978.

Cora Diamond, 'Eating meat and eating people', *Philosophy*, 53, 1978.

G.R. Dunstan, *Malcolm Millar Lecture*, 1981, 'Therapy and care: psycho-dynamic and theological images of man', University of Aberdeen.

G.R. Dunstan, *The first Charles Westley-Hume Memorial Lecture*, 1982, 'Science and sensibility', Universities' Federation for Animal Welfare.

Gavin J. Fairbairn, 'Complexity and the value of lives: some philosophical dangers for mentally handicapped people', *Journal of Applied Philosophy*, 1991, 8:2.

A.M. Farrer, 'For a marriage', in *A Celebration of Faith*, Hodder & Stoughton, 1970.

A.M. Farrer, 'The Eucharist in I Corinthians', in *Eucharistic Theology Then and Now*, SPCK, Theological collections, 9, 1968.

C.L. Fisher, 'Animals, humans and x-men: Human uniqueness and the meaning of personhood', *Theology & Science*, 3:3, 2005.

John W. Funder, 'Experiments on animals in medical research', in *Doctors' Decisions*, ed. G.R. Dunstan & E.A. Shinebourne, OUP 1989.

Lori Gruen, 'Animals', in *A Companion to Ethics*, ed. Peter Singer, Blackwells, 1991.

R.F. Holland, 'On behalf of moderate speciesism', *Journal of Applied Philosophy*, 1:2.

Aurel Kolnai, 'The logical paradoxy of forgiveness', *Proceedings of the Aristotelian Society*, 1973–4.

Andrew Linzey, 'Animals' in *Christianity: the Complete Guide*, ed. John Bowden, Continuum, 2005.

C.F.D. Moule, 'Man and Nature in the New Testament: some Reflections on Biblical Ecology', *Ethel M. Wood Lecture*, 1964, University of London, Athlone Press.

T. Nagel, 'What is it like to be a bat?', in *Mortal Questions*, Cambridge University Press, 1979.

Helen Oppenheimer, 'Life after death', *Theology*, Sept 1979.

— 'Ought and is', in *Duty and Discernment*, ed. G.R. Dunstan, SCM Press, 1965.

— 'Ourselves, our souls and bodies', in *Studies in Christian Ethics*, 4:1, 1991.

— 'Mattering', in *Studies in Christian Ethics*, 8:1, 1995.

— 'The truth-telling animal', in *Dumbing Down*, ed. Ivo Mosley, Imprint Academic, 2000.

Index

Ronald Preston, 'Christian ethics' in *A Companion to Ethics*, ed. Peter Singer, Blackwell, 1991.

Bertrand Russell, 'A free man's worship', *Mysticism and Logic*, Allen & Unwin, 1917.

Gilbert Ryle, 'A rational animal', *Auguste Comte Memorial Lecture*, 1962, published in *Collected Papers*, Hutchinson, 1971, Vol. II, *Collected Essays 1929–68*.

Sue Savage-Rumbaugh, William M. Fields & J. Taglialatila, 'Language, speech, tools and writing: A cultural perspective', *Journal of Consciousness Studies*, 8:5–7, 2001.

Barbara Smuts, 'Encounters with animal minds', *Journal of Consciousness Studies*, 8:5–7, 2001.

Dorothy Yamamoto, 'Patrolling the boundary' in *Animals on the Agenda*, ed. Andrew Linzey and Dorothy Yamamoto, SCM Press, 1998.

Hume 85
Humpty Dumpty 85

Isaiah 82

Jambo
Jenkins, D. 85
Job 39
Joel 126
Johanson, D.C. & M.A. Edey 35, 46
Johnson, Dr 88
Johnstone-Scott, R. 96

Kant 16, 98, 110
Keats 64
Keller, H. 79
Kenny, A.P. 108
Keynes, J.M. 99
Kipling 107
Köhler, W. 134
Kolnai, A. 120

D. Lambert 134
Lazarus 62
Leakey, R. 91
  & R. Lewin 6, 46, 47, 92
Lewis, C.S. 58, 62
Liebermann, P. 91
Linden, E. 78
Linzey, A. 134, 135, 136
  & D. Cohn-Sherbok 17
Lorenz, K. 56, 68-9, 77, 78, 111, 118
Lovejoy, A.O. 33, 46
Luther 62

Madonna, The 128
Micah 130
Michelangelo 108
Midgley, M. 25, 56, 69, 92
Milton 43
Mitchell, B. 45
Mithen, S. 134
Moses 59, 81
Moule, C. 94
Mozart 28, 51, 93, 108, 121
Muir, Edwin 79, 80, 114

Nagel, T. 41
Newton 92
Nightingale, Florence 90
Nygren, A. 47, 60, 61-3, 64

Otto, R. 129, 131

Paul, St 20, 33, 35, 54, 64, 74, 94, 124-5, 132

Peter, St 36
  Peter, James & John 62, 81
Plato 97
Plotinus 84
Potter, B. 97
Preston, R. 11
Price, H.H. 79, 80

Quick, O. 131

Raphael 128
Regan, T. 19, 37, 96, 97, 111
Russell, B. 73
Ryle, G. 31-2, 37, 72, 95

Samuel 82
Savage-Rumbaugh, S. et al. 80
Sewell, A. 96
Shakespeare 6, 8, 1, 7, 91, 97, 105, 108, 116, 126
Sharpe, L. 15, 35, 52, 69, 80, 111
Shaw 119
Shelley 21
Singer, P. 4, 11, 52
Smuts, B. 137
Socrates 108
Solomon 95, 101
Stephen, St 121
Strawson, P. 72

Tennyson 87
Terence 23, 26
Thomas the Apostle, St 44
Traherne 47, 63, 118, 119, 132

Uhlenbroek, C. 70, 77, 80, 101, 106

van Gogh 108

Washoe 78
Watts, I. 109, 127
Wesley, C. 109
Wordsworth 40, 48, 88, 93, 94, 106
Wittgenstein, L. 79
Woolf, V. 96

Yamamoto, D. 25
Yeats, W.B. 73
Young, G.M. 97

Zeus 138

SOCIETAS

essays in political and cultural criticism

imprint-academic.com/societas

SOCIETAS: essays in political and cultural criticism

Public debate has been impoverished by two competing trends. On the one han
the trivialization of the media means that in-depth commentary has given way to th
ten second soundbite. On the other hand the explosion of knowledge has increase
specialization, and academic discourse is no longer comprehensible. As a result wr
ing on politics and culture is either superficial or baffling.

This was not always so — especially for political debate. The high point of th
English political pamphlet was the seventeenth century, when a number of sma
printer-publishers responded to the political ferment of the age with an outpouring •
widely-accessible pamphlets and tracts. But in recent years the tradition of the poli
cal pamphlet has declined—with most publishers rejecting anything under 100,0C
words. The result is that many a good idea ends up drowning in a sea of verbosi•
However the introduction of the digital press makes it possible to re-create a mo•
exciting age of publishing. *Societas* authors are all experts in their own field, but th
essays are for a general audience. Each book can be read in an evening. The bool
are available retail at the price of £8.95/$17.90 each, or on bi-monthly subscriptic
for only £5/$10. Details/updated schedule at **imprint-academic.com/societas**

IMPRINT ACADEMIC, PO Box 200, Exeter, EX5 5YX, UK
Tel: (0)1392 841600   Fax: (0)1392 841478   sandra@imprint.co.uk